U0525784

King Lear

··❦·· 莎翁戏剧经典 ··❦··

李尔王

〔英〕威廉·莎士比亚 著
张信威 注释

2016年·北京

威廉·莎士比亚

图 1

图 2（见 4 页）

Enter KENT, GLOUCESTER, *and* EDMUND.

Kent. I thought the king had more affected the Duke of Albany than Cornwall.

图 3（见 12 页）

Lear. Peace, Kent!
　　Come not between the dragon and his wrath.
　　I lov'd her most, and thought to set my rest
　　On her kind nursery. Hence, and avoid my sight!
　　So be my grave my peace, as here I give
　　Her father's heart from her! ...

图 4（见 26 页）

Enter EDMUND, *with a letter*.

Edmund. Thou, Nature, art my goddess; to thy law
My services are bound. ...

图 5（见 46 页）

Lear. Do you bandy looks with me, you rascal?

            [*Striking him*.

Oswald. I'll not be struck, my lord.

Kent. Nor tripped neither, you base football player.

            [*Tripping up his heels*.

图 6（见 86—88 页）

Kent. Good king, that must approve the common saw,
Thou out of heaven's benediction comest
To the warm sun.
...
All weary and o'er-watch'd,
Take vantage, heavy eyes, not to behold
This shameful lodging.
Fortune, good night, smile once more; turn thy wheel! [*He sleeps.*

图 7（见 98 页）

Regan. I am glad to see your highness.
Lear. Regan, I think you are; I know what reason
  I have to think so: if thou shouldst not be glad,
  I would divorce me from thy mother's tomb,
  Sepulchring an adultress.

图 8（见 112 页）

Cornwall. Shut up your doors, my lord; 'tis a wild night:
My Regan counsels well; come out o' the storm.

图 9（见 114 页）

A storm, with thunder and lightning. Enter
KENT *and a* Gentleman, *meeting.*

Kent. Who's here, beside foul weather?
Gentleman. One minded like the weather, most unquietly.

图 10（见 118 页）

Enter LEAR *and* Fool.

Lear. Blow, winds, and crack your cheeks! rage! blow!
  You cataracts and hurricanoes, spout
  Till you have drench'd our steeples, drown'd the cocks!

图 11（见 130 页）

Enter EDGAR *disguised as a madman*.

Edgar. Away! the foul fiend follows me!
　Through the sharp hawthorn blow the winds.
　Hum! go to thy cold bed and warm thee.
Lear. Didst thou give all to thy two daughters?
　And art thou come to this?

图 12（见 140 页）

Fool. Prithee, nuncle, tell we whether a madman be a gentleman or a yeoman!

Lear. A king, a king!

图 13（见 144—146 页）

Lear. Then let them anatomize Regan, see what breeds about her heart. Is there any cause in nature that makes these hard hearts? …

图 14（见 156 页）

Third Servant. Go thou; I'll fetch some flax, and
 whites of eggs,
 To apply to his bleeding face. Now, heaven help him!

图 15（见 158 页）

Edgar. Yet better thus, and known to be contemn'd.
Than still contemn'd and flatter'd. ⋯

图 16（见 176 页）

Cordelia. Alack! 'tis he: why, he was met even now
 As mad as the vex'd sea; singing aloud;
 Crown'd with rank fumiter and furrow weeds,
 With burdocks, hemlock, nettels, cuckoo-flowers,
 Darnel, and all the idle weeds that grow
  ...

图 17 (见 194 页)

Lear. I will die bravely as a bridegroom. What! I will be jovial; come, come; I am a king, My masters, know you that?

图 18（见 206 页）

Cordelia. O! look upon me, sir,
 And hold your hands in benediction o'er me,
 No, sir, you must not kneel.

图 19（见 208 页）

Kent. Report is changeable. 'Tis time to look about; the powers of the kingdom approach apace.

图 20（见 210 页）

Enter, with drum and colours, EDMUND, REGAN,
Officers, Soldiers, *and others.*

Edmund. Know of the duke if his last purpose hold,
Or whether since he is advis'd by aught
To change the course; ...

图 21（见 216 页）

Edgar. Here, father, take the shadow of this tree
   For your good host; pray that the right may thrive.
   If ever I return to you again,
   I'll bring you comfort.

图 22（见 234 页）

Albany. Produce the bodies, be they alive or dead:
   This judgment of the heavens, that makes us tremble,
   Touches us not with pity.

图 23（见 240—242 页）

Edgar. Look up, my lord.
Kent. Vex not his ghost: O! let him pass; he hates him
    That would upon the rack of this tough world
    Stretch him out longer.

"莎翁戏剧经典"丛书总序

莎士比亚(William Shakespeare,1564—1616)是英国 16 世纪文艺复兴时期的伟大剧作家和诗人,也是世界文坛上的巨擘。他一生创作了 38 部戏剧作品(一说 37 部),诗作包括两部长篇叙事诗、一部十四行诗集以及其他一些短篇诗作。四百多年来这些作品被翻译成多种文字,在世界各地广泛传播。正如他同时代的批评家和剧作家本·琼生所说,他是"时代的灵魂","不属一个时代,而属于所有的时代!"莎士比亚在世期间,他的戏剧作品曾吸引了大量观众,包括宫廷王室成员和普通百姓,产生了巨大影响。18 世纪以来,这些作品始终活跃在舞台上,20 世纪随着电影业的发展,它们又被搬上银幕。几百年来,无论是体现莎士比亚原作的表演还是经过不断改编的作品,莎剧都拥有众多的观者,散发出不灭的艺术光辉;另一方面,自 1623 年莎士比亚全集第一对开本问世,莎士比亚的戏剧也成为学者和广大普通读者阅读、学习、研究的对象,在历代读者的阅读和研究中,这些作品不断得到新阐释和挖掘。莎士比亚的作品焕发着永久不衰的生命活力。

1564 年 4 月,莎士比亚出生于英格兰中部的埃文河畔的斯特拉福镇。家境殷实,父亲曾经营手套和羊毛,并做过小镇的镇长。莎士比亚小时曾在镇上的文法学校读书,受到过较为正规的拉丁文和古典文学的教育。不久,家道中落,陷入经济困境,这可能成为莎士比亚后来未能进入大学读书的原因。1582 年,莎士比亚十八岁时与邻村一位大他八岁的女子安·哈撒韦成婚,六个月后,大女儿苏珊娜降生,此后他们又有了一对孪生子女,不幸的是,儿子哈姆内特早夭。16 世纪 90 年代左右,莎士比亚来到伦敦,发展他的戏剧事业。他曾是剧团的演员、编剧和股东。90 年代初期,莎士比亚即开始戏剧创作。1592 年,莎士比亚已在同行中崭露头角,被当时的"大学才子"剧作家格林所嫉妒,他把莎士比亚称作"那只新抖起来的乌鸦","借我们的羽毛来打扮自己……狂妄地幻想着能独自震撼(shake-scene)这个国家的舞台"。1592—1594年间,伦敦因流行瘟疫,大部分剧院关闭,在此期间莎士比亚完成了两部著名的长篇叙事诗《维纳斯与阿多尼斯》与《鲁克丽丝受辱记》。1594年剧院恢复营业之后,莎士比亚加入宫廷大臣剧团,并终生服务于该剧团,直到1613年离开伦敦返回家乡。16世纪90年代中期,他进入了戏剧创作的巅峰时期。在1590年至1613年的二十多年之间,莎士比亚共创作了历史剧、悲剧、喜剧、传奇剧等38部。16世纪90年代中后期,他的创作以喜剧和历史剧为主,包括喜剧《仲夏夜之梦》(1595)、《威尼斯商人》(1596)、《无事生非》(1598—1599)、《皆大欢喜》(1599—1600)等和大部分历史剧,如《理查三世》(1592—1593)、《亨利四世》(上、下)(1596—1598)、《亨利五世》(1598—1599)等。这一时期,他的创作风格较为明快,充满积极向上的格调,即便剧中有悲剧的成分,整个作品也透露出对生活的肯定,对理想的向往,如《罗密欧与朱丽叶》(1595)。进入17世纪后,莎士比亚的戏剧更多地转向对人生重大问题的思考,探索解决人生之困顿的途径,诸如权力、欲望、嫉妒、暴政等等。四大悲剧《哈姆莱特》(1600—1601)、《奥瑟罗》(1603—1604)、《李尔王》(1605—1606)、《麦克白》(1606)均完成于这一时期。此外,几部重要的罗马题材剧也在16世纪90年代末和新世纪的最初几年完成,如《裘力·凯撒》(1599)、《安东尼与克里奥佩特拉》(1606)、《科里奥兰纳斯》(1608)等。莎士比亚这一时期也创作了几部喜剧,但风格较前一时期更多悲情色彩,更为沉重而引人深思。1609年,莎士比亚《十四行诗集》出版。晚期的莎士比亚剧作风格有一定变化,最有影响的是传奇剧,如《暴风雨》,通过想象的世界与现实世界的对照来探讨人生问题。

莎士比亚的名字开始传入中国是在19世纪中上叶,他的戏剧被翻译成汉语而为国人所知则是在20世纪初期。当时,他剧作的内容通过英国19世纪兰姆姐弟《莎士比亚戏剧故事集》的汉译被介绍到中国来,即无译者署名的《澥外奇谭》(1903)和林纾、魏易翻译的《吟边燕语》(1904)。20世纪20年代,莎剧汉译事业的开拓者田汉翻译了《哈孟雷特》(1921)和《罗密欧与朱丽叶》(1924)。此后,朱生豪、梁实秋、孙大雨、曹禺、曹未风、虞尔昌等译家都翻译过莎士比亚的剧作。朱生豪先生在经历日本侵略的苦难、贫穷和疾病折磨的极其艰苦的环境下,以惊人的毅力和顽强的意志,克服种种艰难险阻,穷毕生之精力完成了31部半莎剧的翻译,成为播撒莎士比亚文明之火的普罗米修斯,译莎事业的英雄和圣徒。他的莎剧译文优美畅达,人物性格鲜明,成为广大读者所珍爱的艺术瑰宝。梁实秋是中国迄今为止唯一一位个人独立完成莎剧和莎诗汉译工程的翻译家。梁译有详尽的注释和说明,学术含量较高。1956年,卞之琳翻译的《哈姆雷特》出版,他完善了孙大雨提出的翻译原则,提出"以顿代步、韵式依原诗、等行翻译"的翻译方法,可谓开一代诗体译法之风,他的译本至今都被视作该剧最优秀的译本。方平是另一位重要的成绩卓著的莎剧翻译家。2000年由他主编主译的《新莎士比亚全集》出版,其中25部莎剧由方平翻译,其他作品由阮坤、吴兴华、汪义群、覃学岚、屠岸、张冲等译出,为国内目前首部全部由分行诗体翻译的莎剧莎诗全集。

时至今日,莎士比亚的戏剧作品仍不断有新的译本出版,对广大读者而言,阅读汉译的莎剧已经是一件十分方便的事情,而这些汉译莎剧作品中不乏优秀的译本。然而,尽管莎剧的汉译丰富多彩,莎剧的改编层出不穷,要想真正了解莎剧的本来面目,我们还需要回到莎剧原文本身。其中的原因有三。一、每一种语言都是丰富的,其表达的意义可能是多元多面的,但由于译出语和译入语两种语言之间的差异,再好的翻译也只能尽可能地贴近原文而不可能百分之百地再现原文的魅力,因此,阅读再好的译本也无法取代或等同于阅读原作;二、莎士比亚生活的时代距今已经有约400年,他所使用的英语与今天人们所熟悉的英语已有较大差异,当时的人们所熟悉的文化和历史事件也是我们今天并不熟知的,因此,要真正领悟他的作品,还需回到他那时的语言和文化中去;三、莎剧经过约400年的变迁,在改编中不断变换,有些已经走出了莎士比亚时代的莎剧,因而,想要认识和了解莎剧,最佳的办法还是回到莎剧的原文本中去。

  莎士比亚生活和创作的时期在16世纪末17世纪初。英语在当时已经得到极大的发展,十分活跃而成熟,尤其莎士比亚戏剧中所运用的英语,文辞丰富、结构灵活、表达力很强。但随着时代的发展,其中的一些用词、用语以及语义等都发生了变化,与我们今天的英语存在一定距离,理解起来也就会有一定困难。莎剧在绝大多数情况下采用的是诗体写作,即人物的语言是分行的,每行十个音节,轻重音节相间,一轻一重的每两个音节构成一个音步,不押韵,因此,他的剧作均为抑扬格五音步的素体诗。这样的诗体形式突显出莎剧语言的艺术魅力,音韵优美、铿锵,节奏感强,表达生动有力。然而,正因为这是诗体写作,在语法上就可能出现诗语言特有的结构,比如倒装句或词序颠倒的现象等。莎剧的语言丰富多彩,不同人物的话语呈现出多种特色,时而体现出古典拉丁语的文风,时而出现双关语、俚语、隐喻等修辞手法。典故、历史事件、政治元素、宗教、生活习俗等等都可能成为今天的读者理解莎剧原文本的障碍。因而,借助良好的注释来理解莎剧的原作就成为我们了解和认识莎剧原貌的必要手段。这次由商务印书馆隆重推出的"莎翁戏剧经典"丛书,重点选出莎士比亚的12部经典剧作,在裘克安先生主编的"莎士比亚注释"丛书的基础上进行了改编修订,并加入了精美的插图。裘先生主编的"莎士比亚注释"丛书对莎剧原文做了多方面的详尽注释,对理解原文起到有效作用,在读者中有较广泛的影响。相信这套"莎翁戏剧经典"的出版会进一步推动莎剧在广大读者中的影响力,提高人们对阅读莎剧以及经典文学作品原文的兴趣和能力,产生积极的和广泛的影响。

屠岸 章燕
2013年10月4日

"莎士比亚注释"丛书总序

莎士比亚研究在新中国有过不平坦的道路和坎坷的命运。解放后不久,大家纷纷学俄语,学英语的人数骤减。研究英国文学,要看苏联人怎么说。"文革"十年,莎士比亚同其他西方"资产阶级"作家一样被打入冷宫。改革开放以后,1978年人民文学出版社出版了在朱生豪译文基础上修订补足的《莎士比亚全集》。随之又出版了一些个别剧的不同译本,如方平译的《莎士比亚喜剧五种》(1979年)和卞之琳译的《莎士比亚悲剧四种》(1988年)。梁实秋的译本,现在大陆上也可以读到了。评介和研究莎士比亚的文章,从"文革"结束后才逐渐多起来。

但是,目前多数人学习、欣赏和研究莎士比亚,是通过中译文来进行的。精通英语而研究莎士比亚的学者不是没有,然而他们人数不多,年纪却老迈了。最近若干年,才有一些年轻人到英国或美国去学习和研究莎士比亚。

1981年我就想到有必要在中国出版我们自己注释的莎士比亚著作。谈起来,许多朋友都赞成。1984年中国莎士比亚研究会筹备和成立时,我自告奋勇,联系了一些志同道合的学者,共同开始编写莎士比亚注释本。商务印书馆大力支持出版这套丛书。到2002年底已出书26种,而且第一次印刷版已全部售完。这证明这套丛书是很受欢迎的。

要知道,莎士比亚是英语文学中最优秀的代表人物,他又是英语语言大师,学习、欣赏和研究他的原著,是译文无法替代的。商务印书馆以其远见卓识,早在1910年和1921—1935年间,就出版过几种莎士比亚剧本的注释本,以满足这方面的需求。那时的教会学校学生英文水平高,能读莎著;不但大学生能读,连有些中学生都能读。可从那时以后,整整50年中国就没印过原文的莎士比亚著作。

世界各国,莎著的注释本多得不计其数。如果唯独中国没有,实在说不过去。如果没有,对于中国知识分子欣赏和研究莎士比亚十分不利。近年来,中国人学英语的越来越多了,他们的英文水平也逐渐提高了。因此,也存在着一定的读者市场。

有了注释本,可以为明天的莎士比亚研究提供一个可靠的群众基础。而译本显然不能提供可靠的基础。

莎士比亚是16、17世纪之交的作者,他写的又是诗剧。对于现代的读者,他的英语呈现着不少的困难。不要说掌握了现代英语的中国读者,就是受过一般教育的英美人士,在初读莎士比亚原著时也面临许多障碍,需要注释的帮助。

莎士比亚的时代,英语正从受屈折变化拘束的中世纪英语,向灵活而丰富的现代英语转变。拉丁语和法语当时对英语影响很大。而莎士比亚对英语的运用又有许多革新和创造。主要的困难可以归纳为以下几个方面,也就是注释要提供帮助的方面:

(一)词汇。许多词虽然拼法和现在一样,但具有不同的早期含义,不能望文生义。另有一些词拼法和现在不一样,而含义却相同。莎士比亚独创了一些词。他特别喜欢用双关语,在他创作的早期尤其如此。而双关语是无从翻译的。这是译本无论如何也代替不了注释本的原因之一。

让我们举《哈姆莱特》剧中男主角出场后最初讲的几句话为例:

King:But now, my cousin Hamlet, and my son —
Hamlet〔Aside〕:A little more than kin, and less than kind!
King:How is it that the clouds still hang on you?
Hamlet:Not so, my lord. I am too much i' the sun.

• 梁实秋的译文如下:

王:现在,我的侄子哈姆雷特,也是我的儿子,——
哈[旁白]:比侄子是亲些,可是还算不得儿子。
王:怎么,你脸上还是罩着一层愁云?
哈:不是的,陛下;我受的阳光太多了。

- 卞之琳的译文如下：
  王：得，哈姆雷特，我的侄子，我的儿——
  哈［旁白］：亲上加亲，越亲越不相亲！
  王：你怎么还是让愁云惨雾罩着你？
  哈：陛下，太阳大，受不了这个热劲"儿"。
- 朱生豪的译文如下：
  王：可是来，我的侄儿哈姆莱特，我的孩子——
  哈［旁白］：超乎寻常的亲族，漠不相干的路人。
  王：为什么愁云依旧笼罩在你的身上？
  哈：不，陛下；我已经在太阳里晒得太久了。

这里，主要困难在于莎士比亚让哈姆莱特使用了 kin 和 kind 以及 son 和 sun 两组双关语。kind 一词又有双关意义，翻译无法完全表达，只能各译一个侧面。结果，梁和卞两先生还得用注释补足其义，朱译则连注释也没有。这种地方，能读原文注释本的人才能充分领略莎氏原意。

哈姆莱特在旁白里说：比亲戚多一点——本来我是你的侄子，现在又成了你的儿子，确实不是一般的亲戚关系啊；然而却比 kind 少一点——kind 有两层意思，一是"同类相求"的亲近感，一是"与人为善"的善意感，我同你没有共同语言，我也不知道你是安的什么心。这话只能对自己说，在舞台上假定对方是听不到的。哈姆莱特的第二句话是公开的俏皮话：哪里有什么阴云呀，我在太阳里晒得不行呢。sun 是跟 clouds 相对；太阳又意味着国王的恩宠，"你对我太好了，我怎么会阴郁呢？"sun 又跟 son 谐音，"做你的儿子，我领教得够了。"原文并不是像梁实秋所说的那样晦涩难解。可是含义太复杂，有隐藏的深层感情，所以无法译得完全。

（二）语法。有些现象，按现代英语语法的标准看，似乎是错误的，但在当时并不错，是属于中世纪英语的残余因素。例如有些动词过去分词的词尾变化、代词的所有格形式、主谓语数的不一致、关系代词和介词的用法等方面，都有一些和现在不同的情况。注释里说明了，可以举一反三去理解。

（三）词序的颠倒和穿插。词尾屈折变化较多的中世纪英语本来对词序没有严格的要求。伊丽莎白时代继承了这种习惯。同时，诗的节律和押韵要求对词序作一定的灵活处理。莎士比亚的舞台语言以鲜明、有力、生动为首要考虑，有时他就把语法和句法放在从属的地位。在激动的台词中，由于思路、感情的变化，语言也常有脱出常规的变化。这些地方，有了注释的指点，理解就容易得多。

（四）典故。莎士比亚用典很多。古希腊、罗马神话，《圣经》故事，英国民间传说，历史逸事……他都信手拈来。其中有一大部分对于英美读者来说乃是常识，但中国读者就很需要注释的帮助。

（五）文化背景。注释可以提供关于基督教义、中世纪传统观点、文艺复兴时期新的主张、英国习俗等方面的知识。

除上述以外，还有莎剧中影射时事，以及版本考据诸问题，在注释本中可以详细论述，也可以简单提及。

世界文豪莫不是语言大师，而要真正理解和欣赏一位大师的文笔，当然非读他的原著不成。出版莎士比亚注释本，首先是为了让中国读者便于买到和读到他的原著。不过我们自知现出的几十种在版本、注释和其他方面还存在不足之处，希望读者多提意见，以便今后不断改进。

裘克安

前　　言

《李尔王》是莎士比亚的四大悲剧之一。20世纪的中外评论家多数同意，它是莎士比亚最伟大的悲剧：个人悲剧、代沟悲剧、社会悲剧、人类悲剧兼而有之，具有强烈的感情冲击力和深刻的思想哲理性。例如，英国评论家弗赖伊（Northrop Frye）在1986年说："对于19世纪和20世纪初期，《哈姆莱特》是莎士比亚的中心戏剧，那时这么多的文化因素都围绕一个问题，即行与知的难于统一；而到了本世纪的存在主义时期，虽然那个问题仍旧突出，人们却越来越感到企图使这个为掠夺性统治者建立的世界理性化乃是荒诞的，于是《李尔王》开始移到中心位置，取代了《哈姆莱特》。"这段话的意思，到下面再说。

威廉·莎士比亚（William Shakespeare，1564—1616）的详细生平，请见我编著的《莎士比亚年谱》。他生活于英国文艺复兴时代晚期，即英国综合国力因资本主义兴起而迅速上升的初期。他出生在英格兰中部小镇斯特拉福德一个手工业主家庭。学历很浅，主要靠自学成才。22岁时来到繁华的首都伦敦。传说开始在剧院门口为有钱的看客照料马匹，后来逐步成为著名戏班子的杂役、演员、剧作家和股东。他十分勤奋善学，从社会各阶层吸收丰富的生活资料和语言资料，很快从模仿走上创作和不断试验创新的文学道路。他写了两首叙事长诗和一系列十四行诗，献给贵族，公开出版，或在文人雅士之间传阅，为此赢得颇高的诗圣名。但他更喜爱创作戏剧——以无脚韵诗（blank verse）为主的诗剧。他不断提高情节、人物、诗句创作的水平，刻意铸造每一剧本不同的风格和意境。早期作品以喜剧为多，继之发展了系列的英国历史剧。中年熟谙世故人情之后，深入发掘不同人的性格的深层结构。用行动、言语和人物之间的相互关系,巧妙地揭示人的心灵的奥秘和发展变化,提出了众多人生的问题。在创作了《哈姆莱特》和《奥瑟罗》之后,大约于1605年写了《李尔王》,那时莎士比亚本人41岁。

英国国王詹姆斯一世的宫廷喜庆记事册上记载着:1606年12月26日,"国王供奉剧团"(即莎士比亚所在的剧团)于圣斯蒂芬之夜在白厅为国王陛下演出悲剧《李尔王》。

1607年11月26日,《李尔王》在书业公所登记。书业公所是当时出版商和印刷商的行会组织,统一管理和保护版权(剧本的版权属剧团)。1608年,《李尔王》的第一个四开本出版,其书名页文字如下:

"威廉·莎士比亚绅士著:李尔王及其三个女儿的生活与死亡的真实历史剧。还有葛罗斯特伯爵的嗣子爱德伽的不幸身世及装扮成疯乞丐汤姆的可怜相。按圣诞节圣斯蒂芬夜〔即上述1606年12月26日〕在白厅国王陛下前演出本。由常在伦敦岸边寰球剧院演戏的国王陛下的仆从〔即供奉剧团〕演出。为纳撒尼尔·巴特尔印刷,并在他的书店出售,书店以花公牛为记,位于圣保罗教堂前街圣奥斯丁门附近。1608年。"

《李尔王》的故事梗概如下:传说中的古不列颠国王李尔已经80岁了(据传说他生活在公元前800年左右,当时英国为凯尔特民族所居住。《李尔王》实际不是历史剧,莎士比亚在此也并不讲究历史的真实性)。他专权多年,王后早死,没有男嗣,只有三个女儿:长女高纳里尔(已嫁给看似软弱的奥本尼公爵)、次女里根(已嫁给残暴的康华尔公爵)和小女考狄利娅。李尔意欲退位闲居,已内定将国土三分,交给三个女儿去掌管,自己则和最宠爱的小女儿一起住。但在公开的朝廷上,他突然宣布要三个女儿说一说哪一个最爱他,"以便我把最大的一份恩赐交给天性以其美德要求得到的人"(Ⅰ i 51—52)。长女和次女用夸张的阿谀奉承之词骗得李尔王的欢心。小女深知两个姐姐的假心假意,不肯效尤,只是用朴素的语言说,我按应尽的义务爱父亲,将来还要用一半的爱心去爱丈夫,其余没有什么好说的。李尔对此勃然大怒,感到在众人面前下不来台,当场决定把原定给小女的一份国土分给两个长女,剥夺小女的一切遗产,并放逐为小女说情的大臣肯特伯爵。幸好随后了解了情况的法兰西国王发现考狄利娅纯真可爱,将她娶走,离开英国。

放弃了王权的李尔起先到长女处住,他带着100名骑士作扈从。长女本来嫌弃老人,因为他的弄人挨骂而打了长女的侍卫,就更横加指责,要裁撤李尔的一半骑士。李尔气极,咒骂长女,改而投奔次女。

次女得到长女的报信,为避开李尔离家去了葛罗斯特伯爵的城堡,并支持凶狠的丈夫先下手枷了李尔差遣的先行使者(改装的肯特)。当李尔来到,面对了次女和随后赶来的长女的无情责难时,他的怒火越来越旺,并被迫在一个狂风暴雨之夜出走荒原。

在荒野上,暴风雨在继续,李尔饥寒交迫,而心理上的痛苦更为剧烈,思前想后,推己及人,神志忽明忽暗。陪伴他的只有改装的肯特、弄人和装疯的乞丐汤姆。李尔从高位跌下,受到忘恩负义的对待,目睹贫民的苦难,思想大变,自己提出了一系列的疑问,直至人类命运的大问题。

小女考狄利娅听说父亲受虐待,从法国带兵来到英国,为捍卫老父的权利,要向两个姐姐开战。

李尔由肯特护送到法军营帐,小女给他延医,使他在音乐声中入睡。半疯的李尔逐渐醒来,依稀认出了小女儿。他对小女说的一番话十分动人:"我想这位夫人是我的孩子考狄利娅。……请你不要哭泣。……我记得,你的两个姐姐待我不好。你倒有些缘由,她们可没有。……你一定得包涵我。请你现在忘记和宽恕。我是又老又糊涂了。"

战争打响。李尔和小女被俘了,关在英军的监狱里。两个蛇蝎姐妹不但为权力而倾轧,还为夺取年轻投机分子爱德蒙而争风吃醋。高纳里尔毒死了里根,自己也因为阴谋败露而自杀。高纳里尔在死前和奸夫爱德蒙曾下密令让人绞死考狄利娅。后来爱德蒙决斗临死良心发现,但为时已晚,考狄利娅已被绞死。

半疯的李尔捧着考狄利娅的尸身,一方面悲恸于她已僵死,另一方面还幻想她仍有一丝呼吸。在这样的情况下李尔自己也终于死了。

战后的不列颠由后来转弱为强的长婿奥本尼公爵、曾经装扮成疯乞丐的爱德伽以及始终跟随李尔的肯特三人收拾残局。

以上是情节的主线,即李尔王和三个女儿的故事。剧中还有一条辅线,即葛罗斯特伯爵和两个儿子的故事。葛有一个城堡和一份不小的财产,本应传给长子爱德伽,但他另有一个刁钻而又心狠的私生子爱德蒙。后者诬指哥哥企图弑父以便提早占有财产,葛居然轻信私生子,宣布通缉因畏惧外逃的长子。为避人耳目,爱德伽装扮成疯乞丐汤姆,在外流浪,暴风雨中与李尔相遇。

葛罗斯特同情李尔,要出去找他,暗中给予解救,他又收到一封信,得知考狄利娅的军队已在路上。他把这些告诉爱德蒙,却被这私生子向里根和康华尔这对狠毒的夫妇告了密,被视为叛逆,挖出双眼,成为盲人,赶出自己的城堡。假的疯乞丐爱德伽遇到劫余的父亲,心疼地卫护着他,并通过多佛白垩崖上父亲自杀未遂这一幕对他进行启发和安慰。

私生子爱德蒙乘机篡夺了父亲的城堡和伯爵爵位,并为了进一步钻营,同时勾引高纳里尔和里根这两个女人,致使她们互相嫉妒,都要致对方于死地。

疯乞丐爱德伽恢复骑士装束而出现,在决斗中杀死私生子弟弟爱德蒙,为父亲和自己报了仇。

莎士比亚把以上主次两条线索巧妙地组织在一起,相互穿插和对比,大大加强了情节的生动、复杂和深刻意义。

《李尔王》的故事并不是莎士比亚首创的。

李尔王和三个女儿的故事,最初的影子大概是欧洲十分普及的民间故事《灰姑娘》(Cinderella＝Cinder Girl,在苏格兰叫《草衣》Rashin Coatie＝Rush Coat),它有 700 个变种。基本的核心是一个谦虚、朴素、美丽的妹妹遭到两个又丑又坏的(有时是后母带来的)姐姐的嫉妒。她在灶房劳动,受到虐待,后来借仙人之助，嫁了王子。两个姐姐受到惩罚。

其次，关于英国传说历史上的李尔王，在莎士比亚时代已知的各种记述不下 50 种。其中主要的有：蒙茅斯的杰弗里的《不列颠君主史》(Geoffrey of Monmouth: *Historia Regum Brittanniae*, c.1136)；约翰·希金斯编《行政长官宝鉴》(John Higgins: *The Mirror for Magistrates*, Par I, 1574—)；威廉·沃纳的《阿尔比翁的英格兰》(William Warner: *Albion's England*, 1586)；拉斐尔·霍林谢德的《英吉利、苏格兰和爱尔兰编年史》第二增订版(Raphael Holinshed: *Chronicles of England, Scotland and Ireland*, 2nd expanded ed., 1587)；埃德蒙·斯潘塞的长诗《仙后》(Edmund Spenser: *The Faerie Queene*, 2.10.27—32, 1590)等。

莎士比亚此剧的直接来源，则是大约在 1588 年写成，1594 年有上演记录，1594 年登记，1605 年出版的《李尔王真实编年史》(*The True Chronicle History of King Lear*)，作者不明。在该剧和多数其他记述中，故事结局都是李尔复得王位，但莎士比亚的戏却是以悲剧结尾。

在莎士比亚开始写《李尔王》前两年左右，即 1603 年 10 月，英国发生了一件轰动一时的诉讼案，可能对莎氏是有影响的。一个名叫安斯利(Brian Annesley)的人神经有些失常，他的两个大女儿要求法院裁定并证明他已发疯和失去管理自己财产的能力，而小女儿科黛尔(Cordell)则上诉反对这种裁定。有趣的是，这位科黛尔五年后嫁给了莎士比亚的文艺庇护人骚散普顿伯爵的后父，因此是属于莎士比亚所熟悉人的圈子内的。

莎氏悲剧《李尔王》中的辅线，即葛罗斯特和两个儿子的故事，其来源则是菲利普·西德尼的散文传奇《阿开迪亚》(Philip Sidney: *Arcadia*, II 10, 1590)。其中一个年老的废王听信私生子的谗言，把嗣子判了死罪。私生子篡了王位；老王眼瞎了，嗣子保护和引导他，阻止了他从山顶上跳崖自杀。最后坏蛋被逐，老王回到朝廷，正式把王冠交给嗣子，自己心竭而终。

莎士比亚身后 65 年，内厄姆·泰特(Nahum Tate)把《李尔王》作了大幅度的改编,使此剧有了快乐的结局,教考狄利娅和爱德伽由恋爱而婚配,还删去了弄人一角和法国军队来到英国的情节。这一篡改,主要是认为莎士比亚的剧太悲了,缺乏"诗的正义"(poetic justice,指在一部文学作品里做到恶有恶报,善有善报),要改为"团圆"和"解气"的结局。整个18世纪,英国人大多持这种观点。泰特的篡改本占据了英国舞台150年之久。

到20世纪,人们才勇于正视、接受并逐渐欣赏莎士比亚所创作的悲剧,还它本来的面目。

《李尔王》首先是李尔个人的悲剧。按照古希腊亚理斯多德的说法,悲剧应描写一位"比一般人好的英雄","他之所以陷于厄运,不是由于为非作歹,而是由于犯了错误"。李尔正是这样一位英雄,他的错误在于主观武断,专横易怒,特别是喜听谄媚的话。孔子曰:"巧言令色,鲜矣仁。"这句话在《论语》里出现两次。又说:"巧言乱德。"又说:"巧言、令色、足恭,左丘明耻之,丘亦耻之。"还给巧言令色的人起了一个名字,叫做"佞(nìng)人"。然而李尔,像许多专权的人一样,就是喜欢巧言令色。其后果是灾难性的。

李尔这位英雄,"比一般人好",好在什么地方?这问题说不清。他经历灾难以后,向小女儿要求宽恕,这是全剧中最动人的一幕。观众和读者为此也容易宽恕李尔的过错。有的西方评论家认为此剧可以叫做"李尔的救赎"(Redemption of Lear),意思是李尔的灵魂经过了彻底改造;一方面,像古希腊亚里斯多德所说,悲剧所引起的怜悯和恐惧使剧中人(以及观众)的感情得到净化;另一方面,像基督教所说,经过考验和锻炼,神的恩典拯救了罪人的灵魂。此外,从李尔周围一些好人对他的尊敬和忠心,反衬出来李尔性格中一定也有一些优良的品质。

"代沟"(generation gap)是一个新名词,莎士比亚当时还没有这个名词。不过亲子之间的关系历来是个问题,特别是在社会发展和变化迅速,出现很多新机遇的时代,像英国十六七世纪之交,亲子矛盾有时就很尖锐。应该指出,当时的英国并没有中国封建大家庭制,也没有儒家忠孝的伦理纲常观念。就李尔和葛罗斯特两个家庭来说，存在着两代人权位和财产交接的问题。英国封建家庭包括王室，实行长子继承制；如无男嗣，女儿也有继承权。像李尔这样分割国土和选择继位者，以及葛罗斯特考虑把爵位和财产交给私生子，这都是属于例外的情况。但子女辈嫌老人久居其位，老而不死，出于野心进行迫退和抢夺，则是屡见不鲜的事。《李尔王》中也偶然提到"孝"的概念，叫 filial duty，更多则是提子女对父辈感恩（gratitude），以及亲子之间天性的（natural）亲和关系（kindness，kinship）。（这里附带说一下，有些中译本把 nature 派生的许多词都译做"孝道"，那是容易引起误解的。）

然而无论李尔和他的三个女儿也好，葛罗斯特和他的两个儿子也好，互相都不理解：老人不但不理解那些个人欲望极端强烈的新派子女，也不理解那些老派而善良的子女。这是一个悲剧，这方面有些问题引人深思。

莎士比亚"不仅属于他的时代"，但首先还是属于他的时代，属于伊丽莎白一世和詹姆斯一世时代的英国。《李尔王》虽然说的是古不列颠国王李尔的事，但剧本中所描写的实际是莎士比亚当代的社会背景。这里的悲剧是权力腐蚀作用和社会不公正所造成的人民的痛苦，特别是贫穷农民的痛苦。封建采邑经济破产，征战和赋税加给人民的负担，圈地运动（它本身是不可抗拒的经济发展趋势）迫使农民离开土地，政府一再颁布禁止乞丐和游民，捉到三次便处死刑的严酷法令：这些情况在《李尔王》中都有反映。李尔正是跳出自我，看到和想到穷人处于水深火热之中，产生社会同情，才扩大自己的视野和思想境界的。

莎士比亚并没有，也不可能进行科学的阶级分析，或者追究社会悲剧的政治经济制度的根源，或者提出什么改造社会的方案。他只是模糊地同情当时一些乌托邦社会主义者如托马斯·莫尔（Thomas More，1478—1535）的感情和想法。除了主要用形象思维再现社会现象图景以外，莎士比亚的悲剧反映出当代人们在政治、社会、伦理、哲学领域的许多复杂的思想进步和矛盾。

例如,自然观。Nature这个字及其派生词在《李尔王》中出现不下40余次。这个词一词多义,可译"自然"、"天性"、"人性"等,有时是双关而不可能全部译出其多层次的意义。欧洲中世纪基督教的传统自然观,以古罗马的波伊修斯(Boethius, 480—524)和托马斯·阿奎那斯(Thomas Aquinas, 1225—1274)为代表,认为客观世界为一大宇宙(macrocosm),人体为一小宇宙(microcosm),都是神造的和谐而有秩序的系统,其正常情况是真、善、美的。人为万物之灵,不过因其始祖亚当和夏娃受魔鬼诱惑犯了原罪(original sin),死后有入地狱的危险,但如向神忏悔,蒙神降恩,死后仍有升天堂的可能。人的天性是善的,有理性的,只要人人循规蹈矩,安于本分,忠君王,尊等级,社会就安宁。英国莎士比亚同代的传统学者如胡克尔(Richard Hooker, 1554—1600)和弗朗西斯·培根(Francis Bacon, 1561—1626)基本上都持这种观点。但到文艺复兴时新兴资产阶级产生了新的观点,如英国有代表性的霍布斯(Thomas Hobbes, 1588—1679)的唯物论和无神论,他认为人性是恶的,由欲望和恐惧所支配,人对人就像狼一样。旧的观念提倡仁爱、忍耐、为最后审判进行准备;新的观念则赤裸裸地追求功利,认为这也是敬神的一种方法,甚至主张纵欲。莎士比亚在《李尔王》中描写了两种人:李尔、考狄利娅、爱德伽、肯特、葛罗斯特属传统派,而爱德蒙、康华尔、高纳里尔、里根则属新派。莎士比亚是剧作家,理应持中立和客观的立场,不过我们所得出的总的印象,莎士比亚似乎是传统派,虽然他也似乎倾向赞成新派关于人人平等这类的观点。

关于"自然观",除了人性之外,还有一个人和自然的关系问题。欧洲中世纪虽然认为人的小宇宙和自然的大宇宙是一致的,但由于当时社会生产力还远不能克服或改造自然,因此往往视大自然为超乎人力之外的冷酷无情的力量。例如,李尔王心中的疯狂和大自然的疯狂(暴风雨)有其一致和呼应之处,但暴风雨对李尔同时也是一种额外的鞭挞和惩罚。与此相比较,关汉卿《感天动地窦娥冤》中,窦娥的冤屈却深深感动了天地,天人有更高度的一致。从这里可以看到中西方对天人关系的看法存在很大区别。

其次,是权力观。旧的观念认为"君权神授"。李尔以为他交了权以后自己还理应受到尊敬。再就是长子继承,别人没有话说。但新派却认为可以夺权,有了权就有了一切。像意大利佛洛伦萨的马基维利(Machiavelli,1469—1527)主张为了夺取和巩固权力,君王可以不择手段;既然被统治者采取恶行,统治者也可以采取恶行;言和行不必一致,也不应一致。马基维利的权术观很早就传到英国,在伊丽莎白时代的许多戏剧里都有反映。马基维利式的人都属于反面角色,但看得出来剧作家都感到这类人物有一种特殊魅力。莎士比亚在这个问题上又是属于传统派。但他似乎认为权力和专权很重要,同时又不应该滥用权力,或者居于权位而软弱无能。至于权力对人的腐蚀作用,以及人怎样能从权力的腐蚀作用下解脱出来,这也是莎士比亚的《李尔王》和其他一些剧本所涉及的问题之一。

《李尔王》中有两场戏写的是李尔王被两个大女儿逐出到荒野上,又逢暴风雨,老王又气又悲,神经逐渐失常,提出一系列对人生、命运和神祇的疑问。这是同《圣经·旧约·约伯记》、屈原《天问》、蔡文姬《胡笳十八拍》属于同一类的探究生之意义和控诉人间不平的惊天动地的篇章。除李尔独白之外,莎士比亚又设置真疯的李尔、假疯的汤姆(爱德伽)和弄人三人之间的疯言狂语,多揶揄、讽刺、意味深长之词。实属世界文学不可多得的神来之笔。

弄人是欧洲中世纪君王朝廷和一部分贵族府邸设立的狎近戏弄之臣(或叫弄臣,中国汉朝也有)。英国一直到十七八世纪仍有之,英文叫做 Court Fools 或 licensed fools。他们得到特许,说话无禁忌,可以开各种玩笑,特别是讲真话,在舞台上则有丑角,英文叫 clown, jester, Harlequin,也可以叫 fool。这些人除了滑稽、逗笑,增添轻松喜剧气氛外,主要也是讲真话。在官样语言之外提供一些不同的看法。他们名为"傻子",其实并不傻。像《李尔王》中的弄人,他常常讲真话,戳穿那些阿谀奉承的假话,他是莎士比亚戏剧中众多丑角里最重要的一个。装疯或真疯,也是伊丽莎白时代戏剧中很受群众欢迎的表演方法。四开本《李尔王》书名全名中特别标明其中有疯乞丐汤姆的戏,就是这个缘故。《李尔王》中的人类悲剧,有了这些艺术手法的帮助和反衬,就越加显得深刻,决不能视为是可有可无的。

经过以上粗略的介绍,我们可以看到《李尔王》是多层次的、更宽阔和更深刻的悲剧。哈姆莱特知易行难(知行难于统一)的问题,主要是一个个人的问题;而李尔的错误和深情则超越个人而富于多方面的象征意义。此所以《李尔王》更难读,或者说,更耐读,即反复读和用不同的读法,每次可以有不同的收获。

进入 20 世纪,随着心理学、人类学、政治经济学的进步,人们对人和社会的了解要复杂和深入多了。以前人们向往和满足于一个封闭的小循环,一个善有善报、恶有恶报的快速结局,所以修改《李尔王》。从 19 世纪进入 20 世纪,人们的社会意识、人类意识提高了,就越来越接受和欣赏莎士比亚原来创作的悲剧了。

前面所引弗赖伊的话,说到存在主义时期,说到世界为掠夺性统治者所设,说到企图作理性解释是荒诞的。这是 20 世纪西方一家之言,但它也确乎代表了悲观主义的一派,他们喜欢《李尔王》。他们对莎士比亚的认识是进了一层。莎士比亚敢于正视事物的复杂性和阴暗面,这些西方评论家看到了莎士比亚超时代的现代性。但他们错在误以为莎士比亚和他们一样是悲观主义者,误以为莎士比亚也满足于认为世界是最荒诞的。

《李尔王》的文本基本上有两种,其间出入比较大。一种是 1608 年的四开本,另一种是 1623 年的对折本。除许多小的出入(拼法、分行、用字、舞台指示等等)以外,所谓较大的出入是对折本删去了四开本中的约 300 行,另外又增添了约 100 行,因此对折本比四开本约短 200 行。

就删的内容而言,主要如 IV iii 整场 55 行是侍臣对肯特叙述考狄利娅读信时的情状。III vi 17—55 行共 39 行,是李尔假装对两个大女儿进行缺席审判的一段。IV ii 31 行以下奥尔巴尼的话共34行。V iii 203行以下爱德伽的话18行。

就增加的内容言，如II iv 45—53弄人的话9行，III ii 79—95弄人的话17行。I ii 109前后，充实了葛罗斯特所说时下人际关系败坏的话。IV vi 165前后李尔关于罪恶镀了金，法律的枪就戳不破的话。V iii 309处李尔"你看见了吗？看她，看，她的嘴唇，看那里，看那里"的话，表明他临死前幻想考狄利娅还有一口气。

1986年英国人斯坦利·威尔斯（Stanley Wells）和美国人加里·泰勒（Gary Taylor）合编新的牛津莎士比亚全集时，兼收了四开本和对折本，把前者称为《李尔王史剧》，后者称为《李尔王悲剧》。他们认为对折本删去一些段落，目的是使剧本更具完整感和增进剧情发展的速度，这是莎士比亚有意为之。

不过，一般莎作编者的做法，这里商务印书馆本也采取的做法，则是把四开本和对折本整合起来，以免遗漏莎士比亚的任何文字。为便了读者去细究四开本和对折本的不同，现将主要的删和加的行码附列于后：

对折本删去四开本的：I ii 95—97,144—150,iii 17—21,iv 135—149,225—228；II ii 137—141；III i 7—15,30＝42,vi 17—54,96—114,vii 99—107；IV i 58—63,ii 31—50,53—59,62—69,iii 1—55（整场），vii 33—36,85—97；V i 11—13,18—19,23—28,iii 39—40,55—60,204—221。

对折本新增加的：I i 39—44,ii 109—114,165—171,iv 317—328；II iv 46—54,139—144；III i 22—29,ii 59—65,vi 12—14,83；IV i 6—9,vi 165—170；V iii 310—311。

请注意，由于散文部分行宽无法一致，所以各种版本的行码有时不免略有出入。

莎士比亚所用的无脚韵诗，或称无韵诗或素体诗（blank verse），每行一般为5个抑扬格的音步，共10音节，如3幕4场28行开始的李尔的话：

Poor ná|ked wrétches,|where- só-|e- ér|you áre,|

 抑 扬 抑 扬 抑 扬 抑扬 抑扬

That bide| the pél-| ting óf| this pi-| t(i)less stórm, |
 抑 扬 抑 扬 抑 扬 抑 扬 抑 扬
How sháll| your hoúse-| less heáds| and ún-| fedsides, |
 抑 扬 抑 扬 抑 扬 抑 扬 抑 扬

但在《李尔王》这些晚期的剧作中，莎士比亚为了充分表达激情，常常越出这种规整的格律，把诗行缩短或者延长，使诗句跨行，造成呼号、气喘、惊愕、或者一泻千里，不可抑止的雄辩气势。在《李尔王》中，我们可以发现莎士比亚利用无韵诗达到随心所欲的许多例子。此外，《李尔王》中还用了许多散文，以及不同小调的诗体，以表达反派角色的论辩、丑角的调侃和疯狂的呓语。

裘克安

1993年9月于北京

KING LEAR

DRAMATIS PERSONAE

Lear, King of Britain.
King of France.
Duke of Burgundy.
Duke of Cornwall.
Duke of Albany.
Earl of Kent.
Earl of Gloucester.
Edgar, Son to Gloucester.
Edmund, Bastard Son to Gloucester.
Curan, a Courtier.
Oswald, Steward to Goneril.
Old Man, Tenant to Gloucester.
Doctor.
Fool.
An Officer, employed by Edmund.
A Gentleman, attendant on Cordelia.
A Herald.
Servants to Cornwall.
Goneril,
Regan, } Daughters to Lear.
Cordelia,
Knights of Lear's Train, Officers, Messengers, Soldiers, and Attendants.
Scene-Britain.

注　释

　　1　**Dramatis Personæ**〈拉丁语〉：Characters of the Drama，剧中人物。

　　2　人名的读音：Lear [liə], Edgar [ˈedgə], Edmund [ˈedmənd], Curan [ˈkjuərən], Oswald [ˈɔswəld], Goneril [ˈgɔnəril], Regan [ˈreigən], Cordelia [ˌkɔːˈdiːliə]。

　　3　**Burgundy** [ˈbəːgəndi]：法国东南部一地区，从前是王国和公国，盛产葡萄酒。英、法等国贵族以其封地为名号。

　　4　**Cornwall** [ˈkɔːnwəl]：英格兰西南端一郡。

　　5　**Albany** [ˈɔːlbəni]：英格兰极北部的旧称，由其原领主 Albanacte 而得名，今已废。

　　6　**Kent** [kent]：英格兰东南部一郡。

　　7　**Gloucester** [ˈglɔːstə]：英格兰西南部一郡。

ACT I

SCENE I

A ROOM OF STATE IN KING LEAR'S PALACE

Enter KENT, GLOUCESTER, *and* EDMUND.

Kent. I thought the king had more affected the Duke of Albany than Cornwall.

Gloucester. It did always seem so to us; but now, in the division of the kingdom, it appears not which of the dukes he values most; for equalities are so weighed that curiosity in neither can make choice of either's moiety.

Kent. Is not this your son, my lord?

Gloucester. His breeding, sir, hath been at my charge: I have so often blushed to acknowledge him, that now I am brazed to it.

Kent. I cannot conceive you.

Gloucester. Sir, this young fellow's mother could; whereupon she grew round-wombed, and had, indeed, sir, a son for her cradle ere she had a husband for her bed. Do you smell a fault?

Kent. I cannot wish the fault undone, the issue of it being so proper.

Gloucester. But I have a son, sir, by order of law, some year elder than this, who yet is no dearer in my account: though this knave came something saucily into the world before he was sent for, yet wass his mother fair; there was good sport at his making, and the whoreson must be acknowledged. Do you know this noble gentleman, Edmund?

Edmund. No, my lord.

ACT I SCENE I

I.i（第一幕第一场，后类推）（以下黑体数字为行码）

1　had more affected：had more affection for, was partial to.

4　the division of the kingdom：李尔显然已私下与 Gloucester 和 Kent 谈过此事，本幕稍后才予以宣布。

5　equalities…weighed：shares are so carefully equalized.

5—6　i. e. the shares (equalities) are so carefully balanced (weighed) that close examination (curiosity) will make neither (duke) to prefer the other's share (moiety).

8　breeding：production, birth. Edmund 是其私生子。　**hath**：has, 古英语和诗体中第三人称单数动词词尾有 s 和 th 两种形式，大体上英格兰北部用 s，南部用 th.　**at my charge**：my responsibility.

10　brazed：hardened, made brazen, 脸皮厚了。

11　conceive：understand. 但 Gloucester 接过这个词，用于另一个意思："怀孕"。

12　could：could conceive.

14　ere：before.

15　smell a fault：detect a sin.

16　issue：双关语 1. result；2. offspring.

17　proper：fine, handsome.

18—19　son,…, by order of law：legitimate son, son born in wedlock.　**some year**：about a year.

20　account：estimation, regard.　**knave**：fellow, 此处带有玩笑口吻，而无贬义。　**something**：somewhat.

23　whoreson：rascal, fellow, 相当于上文的 knave, 但亦带"私生子"之义。

Gloucester. My Lord of Kent: remember him hereafter
as my honourable friend.
Edmund. My services to your lordship.
Kent. I must love you, and sue to know you better.
30 *Edmund.* Sir, I shall study deserving.
Gloucester. He hath been out nine years, and away he
shall again. The king is coming.

Sennet. Enter LEAR, CORNWALL, ALBANY,
GONERIL, REGAN, CORDELIA,
and Attendants.

Lear. Attend the Lords of France and Burgundy,
Gloucester.
Gloucester. I shall, my liege.

[*Exit* .GLOUCESTER.

35 *Lear.* Meantime we shall express our darker purpose.
Give me the map here. Know that we have divided
In three our kingdom; and 'tis our fast intent
To shake all cares and business from our age,
Conferring them on younger strengths, while we
40 Unburden'd crawl toward death. Our son of Cornwall,
And you, our no less loving son of Albany,
We have this hour a constant will to publish
Our daughters' several dowers, that future strife
May be prevented now. The princes, France and Burgundy,
45 Great rivals in our youngest daughter's love,
Long in our court have made their amorous sojourn,
And here are to be answer'd. Tell me, my daughters, —
Since now we will divest us both of rule,
Interest of territory, cares of state,—
50 Which of you shall we say doth love us most?

26 My Lord of Kent: i. e. the Earl of Kent. Gloucester 在向 Edmund 介绍对方的头衔。

28 My services … lordship: I am your servant, my lord.

29 sue: beg.

30 study deserving: try to deserve (your love).

31 out: away from home, abroad. 这话交代了 Edmund 以前从未见过 Kent 的原因。

s.d.(stage direction 舞台指导) **Sennet**: 通报重要人物到来或离去的喇叭声。

33 Attend: Go and wait upon.

34 Liege: lord, sovereign.

Exit〈拉丁语〉: goes out, 下场。

35 we: 这是 Lear 自称,英语称 the royal we,相当于"朕",以下 our, us 等同此。 **express**: show, make known. **darker purpose**: secret intention.

37 fast: firm, fixed.

40 Unburden'd: Unburdened. 撇号 ' 用来标明省略一个元音或辅音,有时是为了省略一个音节。 **son**: son-in-law, Duke of Cornwall.

42 constant: firm. **publish**: make public.

43 several dowers: respective dowries. **that**: so that.

46 amorous sojourn: stay for the purpose of wooing (Cordelia).

48 us: ourselves, 指 Lear 自己。 **both**: 按现代语法应为 all,因为指的是下文的三种负担。

49 Interest: Right, title to (and so, possession of).

50 doth: =does (参见 I.i 8 行中的 hath)。 **doth love**: =loves. 此处 doth 是虚词(expletive),因为诗律要求增加一个音节,并没有现代英语的强调意味。52 行中的 doth 同此。

That we our largest bounty may extend
Where nature doth with merit challenge. Goneril,
Our eldest-born, speak first.

Goneril. Sir, I love you more than words can wield the matter;
55 Dearer than eye-sight, space, and liberty;
Beyond what can be valu'd, rich or rare;
No less than life, with grace, health, beauty, honour;
As much as child e'er lov'd, or father found;
A love that makes breath poor and speech unable;
60 Beyond all manner of so much I love you.

Cordelia. [*Aside.*] What shall Cordelia speak? Love, and be silent.

Lear. Of all these bounds, even from this line to this,
With shadowy forests and with champains rich'd,
With plenteous rivers and wide-skirted meads,
65 We make thee lady: to thine and Albany's issue
Be this perpetual. What says our second daughter,
Our dearest Regan, wife to Cornwall? Speak.

Regan. I am made of that self metal as my sister,
And prize me at her worth. In my true heart
70 I find she names my very deed of love;
Only she comes too short: that I profess
Myself an enemy to all other joys
Which the most precious square of sense possesses
And find I am alone felicitate
75 In your dear highness' love.

Cordelia. [*Aside.*]   Then, poor Cordelia!
And yet not so; since, I am sure, my love's
More richer than my tongue.

Lear. To thee and thine, hereditary ever,
Remain this ample third of our fair kingdom,
80 No less in space, validity, and pleasure,

51 That: So that; In order that.

52 nature: natural or filial love.　**challenge**: claim (such bounty).

54 wield the matter: manage to express.

55 space: the world.

57 with: combined with.

58 found: received, experienced.

59 unable: unequal to expressing it.

60 all…so much: all the qualities of everything I have mentioned.

62 these bounds: this limited piece of territory.　**even**: 相当于 just 的一个语气词。

63 shadowy: shady.　**champains**: open fields.　**rich'd**: enriched, fertile.

64 plenteous: causing plentiful harvest.　**wide-skirted**: far-reaching, extensive.　**meads**: meadows.

65 We make thee lady: I make you mistress (owner) of all these bounds, etc. 注意本句的结构：We…lady 为句子的主要部分,lady 后接这段话开首的 Of.　**thine**: your. thy 在元音前变为 thine. 在当时的英语和以后的诗体中,第二人称单数代词除 you, your, yours 外,还有 thou (主格), thee (宾格), thy (所有格)和 thine (元音前或 h 开始的词前的所有格和名词性物主代词)。按当时的习惯,一般下对上称 you, 上对下称 thou, 对疏者称 you, 对亲者称 thou. 但这并不是固定不变的,关系或情绪变化时,用法也随之而异。　**issue**: descendants.

65—66 to…Be this perpetual: let this belong for ever to.

66 What…daughter: What does our second daughter say. 在当时的英语中,疑问句可以用颠倒主谓次序的办法构成,而不用助动词 do.

68 sister: 后省略 is made of.　**metal**: ①material; ②temperament, 作此义解时现代英语拼作 mettle.

69 prize…worth: I count myself equal to her (in my affection for you).　**In my true heart**: in alll sincerity.

70 names…love: exactly describes my love as it really is.

71 Only…short: 只是她说得还不够。　**that**: in that, because.

73 most precious square of sense: most delicate sense. square 可能指木匠用的矩尺,此处暗指 perfection of sense.

74 alone: only.　**felicitate**: made happy, 动词 felicitate 的过去分词。动词结尾为 te 时,最后的 d 省略。

75 这一诗行由 In your dear highness' love 和 Then, poor Cordelia 两个部分合成,凑满十个音节,故作错位安排。莎剧文体以无韵诗(blank verse, 或译素体诗)为主,夹杂散文、押韵对句(couplet)、格律诗等其他形式。如本剧一开始为散文,指普通交谈。从 Lear 上场后,

Than that conferr'd on Goneril. Now, our joy,
Although our last, not least; to whose young love
The vines of France and milk of Burgundy
Strive to be interess'd; what can you say to draw
85   A third more opulent than your sisters? Speak.
Cordelia. Nothing, my lord.
Lear. Nothing?
Cordelia. Nothing.
Lear. Nothing will come of nothing: speak again.
90 *Cordelia.* Unhappy that I am, I cannot heave
My heart into my mouth: I love your majesty
According to my bond; nor more nor less.
Lear. How, how, Cordelia! mend your speech a little,
Lest you may mar your fortunes.
Cordelia.   Good my lord,
95   You have begot me, bred me, lov'd me: I
Return those duties back as are right fit,
Obey you, love you, and most honour you.
Why have my sisters husbands, if they say
They love you all?
               Haply, when I shall wed,
100   That lord whose hand must take my plight shall carry
Half my love with him, half my care and duty:
Sure I shall never marry like my sisters,
To love my father all.
Lear. But goes thy heart with this?
Cordelia.   Ay, good my lord.
105 *Lear.* So young, and so untender?
Cordelia. So young, my lord, and true.
Lear. Let it be so; thy truth then be thy dower:
For, by the sacred radiance of the sun,
The mysteries of Heacate and the night,
110   By all the operation of the orbs
From whom we do exist and cease to be,

35行起,就用庄严的无韵诗。无韵诗一般每行有十个音节,分为五个抑扬格的音步,即五个前轻后重的两音节单位。但实际上每行中的音节数和音步内轻重音节的安排并非总是很规则的。例如,本行就有十一个音节,可分析如下:
Ĭn yòur|deăr hìgh|nĕss' lòve|Thĕn pòor|Cŏrdèlia|
最后一个音步就多一个轻音节。

76　so:代替 poor.

77　More richer:中世纪英语常用这种 double comparative 来表示强调。

78　thine: yours, your descendants.

78—79 i.e. Let this ample third ... remain hereditary (belong by heredity) for ever to thee and thine.

80　validity: value.

82　to: in.

83 指法兰西国王和勃艮第公爵,因为法国多葡萄园,盛产葡萄酒,而勃艮第多牧场,盛产牛奶。

84　interess'd: interested. interess 是 interest 的旧拼法,源自拉丁文 interesse.

89　of: from, out of.

90 i.e. how unhappy I am that I...

90—91　heave ... mouth: i.e. express in words what is in my heart.

92　bond: duty, obligation.

93　mend: amend, improve.

95　begot: beget 的过去分词,同 begotten,生。　**bred**: breed 的过去分词,养,brought up.

96　are right fit: they are most fit to be returned.

99　all: entirely, only (又见 I.i 103)。　**Haply**: Perhaps.

100　plight: plighted troth, marriage vow.

101　care: concern, attention (又见 I.i 112)。

102　Sure: Surely.

103　To love: If I should love.

104　goes: matches, harmonizes.　**Ay**: yes.

107　dower: dowry.

108　by: 指 ... 为誓。

109　Hecate ['hekit]: 希腊神话中司黑夜和冥界的女神,后人又认为司魔法和巫术。

110　operation: work, influence.　**orbs**: heavenly bodies. 从前人们认为星球能影响人的命运。

111　whom: which.

Here I disclaim all my paternal care,
Propinquity and property of blood,
And as a stranger to my hear and me
115 Hold thee from this for ever. The barbarous Scythian,
Or he that makes his generation messes
To gorge his appetite, shall to my bosom
Be as well neighbour'd, pitied, and reliev'd,
As thou my sometime daughter.
Kent.   Good my liege,—
120 *Lear.* Peace, Kent!
Come not between the dragon and his wrath.
I lov'd her most, and thought to set my rest
On her kind nursery. Hence, and avoid my sight!
So be my grave my peace, as here I give
125 Her father's heart from her! Call France. Who stirs?
Call Burgundy. Cornwall and Albany,
With my two daughters' dowers digest the third;
Let pride, which she calls plainness, marry her.
I do invest you jointly with my power,
130 Pre-eminence, and all the large effects
That troop with majesty. Ourself by monthly course,
With reservation of a hundred knights,
By you to be sustain'd, shall our abode
Make with you by due turn. Only we shall retain
135 The name and all the addition to a king;
The sway, revenue, execution of the rest,
Beloved sons, be yours: which to confirm,
This coronet part between you.
Kent.   Royal Lear,
Whom I have ever honour'd as my king,
140 Lov'd as my father, as my master follow'd,
As my great patron thought on in my prayers,—
Lear. The bow is bent and drawn; make from the

ACT I SCENE I

112 disclaim: renounce.

113 Propinquity: 本意为 nearness，此处作 kinship 解。 **property of blood**: ownership of your blood.

115 Hold … this: Regard you from this time. 语法上接上行中的 as. **Scythian**: 古代居住在黑海以北 Scythia ['siðiə] 平原上的游牧民族，据说有杀父母而食的习俗。

116 he: a man. **generation**: children. **messes**: portions of food.

117 gorge: fill up, satisfy.

118 as well neighbour'd: held as close. **reliev'd**: comforted.

119 sometime: former.

121 i.e. don't try to stop my wrath (cf. 171 行 below). **his**: its.

122 thought: hoped. **set my rest**:双关语 1. stake all my remaining lands (暗喻赌博); 2. depend for my repose.

123 kind nursery: loving care or nursing. **Hence … sight!**: Go away, out of my sight!

124 be … peace: let my grave be my peace.

125 from: away from. **France**: i.e. the King of France. **Who stirs?** Is there no one going to move? 群臣都被李尔的狂怒惊呆了，一时竟无人去执行王命。

127 digest: incorporate, assimilate.

128 Let pride … her: Let her pride find her a husband, i.e. let her find one for herself without a dowry. **plainness**: plain-speaking. 下面 147 行同。

129 invest: endow.

130 large effects: manifestations of splendour.

131 troop with: accompany, are associated with. **by monthly course**: each time for the period of a month.

131—134 此句核心为 Ourself shall make our abode with (live with) you.

132 With reservation of: i.e. While reserving to myself.

133 sustain'd: supported.

134 by due turn: in turn, in rotation.

135 addition: titles, ceremonies. **to**: due to.

136 revenue: 税收等于国家收入。此词在这里按格律重音应落在第二音节上。 **execution**: 行政。

137 sons: sons-in-law.

138 part: divide.

141 on: of.

142 make from the shaft: keep away from the arrow, i.e. do not interfere with what I am doing.

shaft.

Kent. Let it fall rather, though the fork invade
The region of my heart: be Kent unmannerly
145   When Lear is mad. What wouldst thou do, old man?
Think'st thou that duty shall have dread to speak
When power to flattery bows? To plainness honour's bound
When majesty falls to folly. Reserve thy state;
And, in thy best consideration, check
150   This hideous rashness: answer my life my judgment,
Thy youngest daughter does not love thee least;
Nor are those empty-hearted whose low sound
Reverbs no hollowness.

Lear.   Kent, on thy life, no more.

Kent. My life I never held but as a pawn
155   To wage against thine enemies; nor fear to lose it,
Thy safety being the motive.

Lear.   Out of my sight!

Kent. See better, Lear; and let me still remain
The true blank of thine eye.

Lear. Now, by Apollo,—

Kent.   Now, by Apollo, king,
160   Thou swear'st thy goods in vain.

Lear.   O vassal! miscreant!

                            [*Laying his hand on his sword.*

Albany. } Dear sir, forbear.
Cornwall.

Kent. Do;
Kill thy physician, and the fee bestow
Upon the foul disease. Revoke thy gift;
165   Or, whilst I can vent clamour from my throat,
I'll tell thee thou dost evil.

Lear.   Hear me, recreant!
On thine allegiance, hear me!

ACT I SCENE I

143 though…invade: even though the arrowhead enters.

144—145 be…mad: i.e. let Kent be disrespectful (unmannerly) when Lear is mad.

145 What wouldst thou do: What are you going to do. 这里 Kent 以老臣的身份直谏,所以用 thou, thee, thy, 而不用较为恭敬的 you. **wouldst**: would 的第二人称单数形式。

146 Think'st: Thinkest, think 的第二人称单数形式。 **have dread**: be afraid.

148 state: regal power.

149 consideration: deliberation.

150 answer…judgment: let my life answer for (the correctness of) my judgment.

153 Reverbs no hollowness: Does not reverberate hollowly. (英谚):"Empty vessels make the most noise." 此处 hollowness 含义双关语 1. emptiness; 2. insincerity. 整句话意为"不高喊空话者心并非空的"。 **on thy life**: at the risk of your life.

154 held: considered. **pawn**: 国际象棋中的卒,工具。

155 wage against: wage war against.

157—158 let me…eye: keep me always in view, always look to me for advice. **still**: always, for ever. **blank**: 白色的靶心。

159 Apollo: 古希腊神话中的太阳神,也是光明和医药之神。因 Lear 是古代英国国王,当时基督教尚未传到英国,故莎士比亚让他指 Apollo 发誓,不用 by God. 其实古代英国并不信希腊之神。不过 Apollo 司光明和医药,和下文联系,指发誓有讽刺意味。

160 swear'st: swear by, by 省略。 **vassal**: slave. **miscreant**: villain (miscreant 的本义是 infidel, misbeliever).

162 Do: Execute your will.

163—164 the fee…disease: 把原该付医师的钱付给疾病。 **gift**: i.e. of Cordelia's share.

165 Or: Otherwise. **vent clamour**: utter noise.

166 dost: do 的第二人称单数形式。 **recreant**: traitor.

167 On thine allegiance: 凭你对国王应有的忠诚。

Since thou hast sought to make us break our vow,—
Which we durst never yet, — and, with strain'd pride
170 To come betwixt our sentence and our power,—
Which nor our nature nor our place can bear,—
Our potency made good, take thy reward.
Five days we do allot thee for provision
To shield thee from diseases of the world;
175 And, on the sixth, to turn thy hated back
Upon our kingdom: if, on the tenth day following
Thy banish'd trunk be found in our dominions,
The moment is thy death. Away! By Jupiter,
This shall not be revok'd.
180 *Kent.* Fare thee well, king; sith thus thou wilt appear,
Freedom lives hence, and banishment is here.
[*To* CORDELIA.] The gods to their dear shelter take thee, maid,
That justly think'st, and hast most rightly said!
[*To* REGAN *and* GONERIL.] And your large speeches may your deeds approve,
185 That good effects may spring from words of love.
Thus Kent, O princes! bids you all adieu;
He'll shape his old course in a country new.   [*Exit.*
Flourish.Re-enter GLOUCESTER, *with* FRANCE, BURGUNDY, *and* Attendants.
Gloucester. Here's France and Burgundy, my noble lord.
Lear. My Lord of Burgundy,
190 We first address toward you, who with this king
Hath rival'd for our daughter. What, in the least,
Will you require in present dower with her,
Or cease your quest of love?
Burgundy.   Most royal majesty,
I crave no more than hath your highness offer'd.

168　hast：have 的第二人称单数形式。

169　we durst never yet：I have never dared to do before.　**durst**：dare 的古体过去式。　**strain'd**：excessive, forced, unnatural.

170　our power：i.e. to execute the sentence.

171　nor … nor：neither … nor.　**place**：position as king.

172　Our potency made good：My power shown to be (still) valid, to prove my authority.

174　diseases：discomforts, troubles.

175　to turn：i.e. I sentence you to turn.

177　trunk：body.

178　Jupiter：罗马神话中的主神,主人世的命运。

180　sith：since.　**wilt**：will 的古体第二人称单数形式。　**appear**：show thyself.

181　Freedom lives hence：i.e. The home of freedom is elsewhere. 从上行开始一直到 187 行用的是押韵对句,以表示 Kent 面对 Lear 的暴怒仍镇定自若。

182　dear：loving.此行意为 May the gods shelter you lovingly.

183　That：Who.

184　large：grand.　**approve**：confirm, make good, 其宾语为 speeches.

185　That：So that.　**effects**：deeds.

187　shape … course：make his way, old as he is.

Flourish：a blast of trumpets.参见 32 行后,*Sennet* 的注释。

188　Here's：谓语在主语之前常用单数。

190　address toward：speak to.

191　rivall 'd：entered into rivalry, competed.

191—192　What, … her：i.e. What is the lowest amount you will accept as an immediate payment of dowry.

195　　　Nor will you tender less.
　　　　Lear.　　　　　　　　Right noble Burgundy,
　　　　When she was dear to us we did hold her so,
　　　　But now her price is fall'n. Sir, there she stands:
　　　　If aught within that little-seeming substance,
　　　　Or all of it, with our displeasure piec'd,
200　　　And nothing more, may fitly like your Grace,
　　　　She's there, and she is yours.
　　　　Burgundy.　　　　　　　I know no answer.
　　　　Lear. Will you, with those infirmities she owes,
　　　　Unfriended, new-adopted to our hate,
　　　　Dower'd with our curse, and stranger'd with our oath,
205　　　Take her, or leave her?
　　　　Burgundy.　　　　　　Pardon me, royal sir;
　　　　Election makes not up on such conditions.
　　　　Lear. Then leave her, sir; for, by the power that made me,
　　　　I tell you all her wealth. — [*To* FRANCE.] For you, great king,
　　　　I would not from your love make such a stray
210　　　To match you where I hate; therefore, beseech you
　　　　To avert your liking a more worthier way
　　　　Than on a wretch whom nature is asham'd
　　　　Almost to acknowledge hers.
　　　　France.　　　　　　　　This is most strange,
　　　　That she, who even but now was your best object,
215　　　The argument of your praise, balm of your age,
　　　　The best, the dearest, should in this trice of time
　　　　Commit a thing so monstrous, to dismantle
　　　　So many folds of favour. Sure, her offence
　　　　Must be of such unnatural degree
220　　　That monsters it, or your fore-vouch'd affection
　　　　Fall into taint; which to believe of her,
　　　　Must be a faith that reason without miracle

195　tender：offer.

196　hold：esteem, regard.　**so**：i.e.dear (in value), worth a good dowry.

197　is fall'n：has fallen 的旧时说法。

198　aught：anything.　**little-seeming substance**：frail-looking body.

199　piec'd：added (to it).

200　like：please

202　owes：owns.

203　new-adopted to our hate：newly become the object of my hatred.

204　stranger'd with：made a stranger (to us) by. 这里莎士比亚临时将 stranger 用作动词。

206　Election…up：It is impossible to make a choice.

207　the power that made me：指造物主,上帝。

208　For you：As for you.

209—210　I would not…hate：I do not want to go so far from my love of you as to match you to her whom I hate.　**beseech**：前面省略 I.

211　avert your liking：turn your affection.　**a more worthier way**：in a worthier direction, 双重比较级表示强调。

212　nature：拟人化,用阴性。

214　even but：only, 强调用法。　**best object**：favourite.

215　argument：object.　**balm**：soothing comfort.

216　trice：instant.

217　to：as to.　**dismantle**：strip off, take off.

218　Sure：Surely.

220—221　monsters：makes monstrous. 这里莎士比亚临时将 monster 用作动词。　**or**：or else, otherwise.　**your fore-vouch'd…taint**：your previously affirmed affection must have decayed.　**taint**：decay.

221—223　which…me：i.e. To believe the above (offence 等等) about her must take a blind faith, which reason, without a miracle, could never plant in my mind.

Could never plant in me.
Cordelia. I yet beseech your majesty —
If for I want that glib and oily art
225 To speak and purpose not; since what I well intend,
I'll do't before I speak, —that you make known
It is no vicious blot murder, or foulness,
No unchaste action, or dishonour'd step,
That hath depriv'd me of your grace and favour,
230 But even for want of that for which I am richer,
A still-soliciting eye, and such a tongue
That I am glad I have not, though not to have it
Hath lost me in your liking.
Lear. Better thou
Hadst not been born than not to have pleas'd me better.
235 *France.* Is it but this? a tardiness in nature
Which often leaves the history unspoke
That it intends to do? My Lord of Burgundy,
What say you to the lady? Love's not love
When it is mingled with regards that stand
240 Aloof from the entire point. Will you have her?
She is herself a dowry.
Burgundy. Royal Lear,
Give but that portion which yourself propos'd,
And here I take Cordelia by the hand,
Duchess of Burgundy.
245 *Lear.* Nothing: I have sworn; I am firm.
Burgundy. I am sorry, then, you have so lost a father
That you must lose a husband.
Cordelia. Peace be with Burgundy!
Since that respects of fortune are his love,
I shall not be his wife.
250 *France.* Fairest Cordelia, that art most rich, being poor;

ACT I SCENE I

223 beseech：beg，下接 226 行的 that 宾语从句，中间两 dashes 之间为插入语。此插入语非完整句，表示 Cordelia 情绪激动。

224 If for I want：if it is because I lack.　**If**：从句所缺的隐含语为 you are disowning me.

225 purpose：mean, intend to act.　**since**：for.

226 known：后省略 that.

227　i.e. not wickedness, murder or fornication.

228 dishonour'd：dishonourable.

230 But ... richer：But just because I lack those things（指下文的 eye and tongue）without which I am the richer.

231 still-soliciting：continually begging for favour.

233 lost ... liking：made me lose your affection.　**Better thou**：it would have been better if you.

234 Hadst：have 的第二人称单数过去式。

235 tardiness in nature：natural slowness.

236 history：thing.　**unspoke**：unspoken.

238 What say you to：What do you think of.

239 regards：considerations.

240 entire：essential.

242 Give but：If you only give.

246 you：指 Cordelia，转向 Cordelia 说话。

247 Peace be with Burgundy!：一般在道别时的客气话，"祝你平安！"。

248 Since that：since.　**respects**：considerations.

250 art：are，be 的第二人称单数现在式。

Most choice, forsaken; and most lov'd, despis'd!
Thee and thy virtues here I seize upon:
Be it lawful I take up what's cast away.
Gods, gods! 'tis strange that from their cold'st neglect
My love should kindle to inflam'd respect.
Thy dowerless daughter, king, thrown to my chance,
Is queen of us, of ours, and our fair France:
Not all the dukes of waterish Burgundy
Shall buy this unpriz'd precious maid of me.
Bid them farewell, Cordelia, though unkind:
Thou losest here, a better where to find.

Lear. Thou hast her, France; let her be thine, for we
Have no such daughter, nor shall ever see
That face of hers again, therefore be gone
Without our grace, our love, our benison.
Come, noble Burgundy.

[*Flourish. Exeunt* LEAR, BURGUNDY,
CORNWALL, ALBANY, GLOUCESTER,
EDMUND, *and* Attendants.

France. Bid farewell to your sisters.

Cordelia. The jewels of our father, with wash'd eyes
Cordelia leaves you: I know you what you are;
And like a sister am most loath to call
Your faults as they are nam'd. Use well our father:
To your professed bosoms I commit him:
But yet, alas! stood I within his grace,
I would prefer him to a better place.
So farewell to you both.

Regan. Prescribe not us our duties.

Goneril.   Let your study
Be to content your lord, who hath receiv'd you
At fortune's alms; you have obedience scanted,
And well are worth the want that you have wanted.

ACT I SCENE I

251 forsaken 和 **despis'd**：前均省略 being.

253 Be it lawful：Let it be lawful that.

255 inflam'd respect：ardent esteem.

256 thrown to my chance：fallen to my lot.

258 waterish：双关语 1. well-watered, abounding in rivers; 2. poor in spirit, thin-blooded.

259 unpriz'd precious：unappreciated by others, but precious to me.

260 though unkind：though they are unkind to you.

261 losest：lose 的第二人称单数现在式。 **here**：this place. **where**：place elsewhere. here 和 where 此处都作名词用。

265 grace：favour. **benison**：blessing.

268 The jewels：这里是 vocative case. **wash'd**：tear-washed.

269 第二个 you 多余。

270 loath：reluctant.

271 as they are nam'd：by their true names. **use**：Treat.

272 bosoms：love.

273 stood I：If I stood.

274 prefer：advance, recommend.

276 Prescribe not us：Do not prescribe (dictate) to us. **study**：concern, endeavour.

278 At fortune's alms：As a charitable gift of fortune. **scanted**：lacked, omitted to do.

279 well...wanted：well deserve the destitution (want) that has befalllen you, 也有人解作 deserve to suffer the same lack of affection (from your husband) that you have shown (to your father).

280 *Cordelia.* Time shall unfold what plighted cunning hides;
Who covers faults, at last shame them derides.
Well may you prosper!
France. Come, my fair Cordelia.
[*Exeunt* FRANCE *and* CORDELIA.
Goneril. Sister, it is not little I have to say of what most nearly appertains to us both. I think our father
285 will hence to-night.
Regan. That's most certain, and with you; next month with us.
Goneril. You see how full of changes his age is; the observation we have made of it hath not been little: he
290 always loved our sister most; and with what poor judgment he hath now cast her off appears too grossly.
Regan. 'Tis the infirmity of his age; yet he hath ever but slenderly known himself.
Goneril. The best and soundest of his time hath been
295 but rash; then, must we look to receive from his age, not alone the imperfections of long-engraffed condition, but, therewithal the unruly waywardness that infirm and choleric years bring with them.
Regan. Such unconstant starts are we like to have from
300 him as this of Kent's banishment.
Goneril. There is further compliment of leave-taking between France and him. Pray you, let us hit together: if our father carry authority with such disposition as he bears, this last surrender of his will but offend us.
305 *Regan.* We shall further think on't.
Goneril. We must do something, and i' the heat.
[*Exeunt.*

ACT I SCENE I

280 **plighted**: plaited 和 pleated 的异体字, 意为 folded, covered.

281 **Who**: Those who (antecedent to them).　**shame them derides**: shame will laugh them to scorn.

283 **little**: insignificant.

284 **appertains to**: concerns.

285 **will hence**: will go hence.

288 **full...age is**: changeable he is now that he is old.

289 **little**: unimportant.

291 **grossly**: obviously.

293 **slenderly known himself**: known little of his real self.

294 **best 和 soundest**: 后省略 act.　**his time**: the years of his life.

295 **rash**: hot-headed.　**look**: expect.

296—297 **alone**: just.　**long-engraffed**: long-engrafted, deep-rooted.　**condition**: disposition.　**therewithal**: along with it.

298 **infirm...years**: years of physical weakness and proneness to anger.

299 **unconstant starts**: sudden whims, erratic acts, fits of waywardness.　**are we like to have**: are what we are likely to have.

300 **this**: i.e. this start, this sudden act.

301 **compliment**: ceremony, formality.

302 **hit together**: strike a bargain, i.e. agree on a course of action.

303 **carry**: i.e. still wields.　**dispositions**: moods.

304 **last surrender**: latest action of giving up rule.　**his**: i.e. his authority.　**offend**: harm (语意较现在强)。

305 **on**: about.

306 **i' the heat**: in the heat, i.e. at once (cf. 'strike while the iron is hot').

SCENE II

A HALL IN THE EARL OF GLOUCESTER'S CASTLE

Enter EDMUND, *with a letter*.

Edmund. Thou, Nature, art my goddess; to thy law
My services are bound. Wherefore should I
Stand in the plague of custom, and permit
The curiosity of nations to deprive me,
5   For that I am some twelve or fourteen moonshines
Lag of a brother? Why bastard? wherefore base?
When my dimensions are as well compact,
My mind as generous, and my shape as true,
As honest madam's issue? Why brand they us
10   With base? with baseness? bastardy? base, base?
Who in the lusty stealth of nature take
More composition and fierce quality
Than doth, within a dull, stale, tired bed,
Go to the creating a whole tribe of fops,
15   Got 'tween asleep and wake? Well then,
Legitimate Edgar, I must have your land:
Our father's love is to the bastard Edmund
As to the legitimate. Fine word, 'legitimate!'
Well, my legitimate, if this letter speed,
20   And my invention thrive, Edmund the base
Shall top the legitimate:—I grow, I prosper;
Now, gods, stand up for bastards!

Enter GLOUCESTER.

Gloucester. Kent banished thus! And France in choler parted!
And the king gone to-night! subscrib'd his power!
25   Confin'd to exhibition! All this done
Upon the gad! Edmund, how now! what news?

ACT I SCENE II

I. ii

1 Nature：Edmund 把大自然而不是 gods 视作自己的保护神。这说明他的思想已经越出了当时的宗教和社会的规范。另外，英文把"私生子"叫做"natural son". Edmund 这样想也是符合自己的身份的。

2 bound：under obligation.

2—3 Wherefore … custom：Why should I be subject to the curse (plague) of custom.这里 custom 指的是英国实行的长子继承权和对私生子的歧视。Edmund 既非长子又是私生子，当然不可能继承父亲的贵族称号和财产。

4 curiosity of nations：people's fastidiousness. **deprive me**：keep me out of my rights.

5 For that：Because. **moonshines**：months.

6 Lag of：Behind (in coming into the world). **bastard**：私生子，常被视为出身低贱、人品卑劣。Edmund 是在发泄对这种看法的不满。但他错把 bastard 和 base 视作同源词。

7 my dimensions：the proportions of my body. **compact**：packed together, made.

8 generous：noble. **true**：well-proportioned.

9 honest madam's：the true wife's.

11 stealth：secret act. **nature**：natural sexual desire.

12 composition：strength of constitution. **fierce**：vigorous, energetic.

13—14 doth, … , Go …：主语是 composition 和 quality. **dull, stale, tired bed**：指正式夫妻之间的性生活。

14 creating：creation of，注意这种介于 participle 和 gerund 之间的用法。这是过渡时期英语的特征之一。 **fops**：fools.

15 Got：Begotten; Conceived. **'tween**：between.

17 is to：is the same towards.

19 speed：succeed.

20 my invention thrive：my scheme work.

21 top：get the better of.

23 in choler parted：departed in anger. choler 原义为"胆汁"，中世纪认为是人体内四种液体（humours）之一，其余三种为 blood, phlegm 和 melancholy.据说人的性格取决于这几种液体的比例。胆汁过多使人暴躁。

24 to-night：last night. **subscrib'd**：given up, surrendered.

25 Confin'd to exhibition!：Restricted to an allowance of money.

26 Upon the gad!：On the spur of the moment, suddenly (as if pricked by a gad, gad = goad，赶牛用的刺棒) **how now!**：how are things?

Edmund. So please your lordship, none.

[*Putting up the letter.*

Gloucester. Why so earnestly seek you to put up that letter?

Edmund. I know no news, my lord.

Gloucester. What paper were you reading?

Edmund. Nothing, my lord.

Gloucester. No? What needed then that terrible dispatch of it into your pocket? the quality of nothing hath not such need to hide itself. Let's see; come; if it be nothing, I shall not need spectacles.

Edmund. I beseech you, sir, pardon me; it is a letter from my brother that I have not all o'er-read, and for so much as I have perused, I find it not fit for your o'er-looking.

Gloucester. Give me the letter, sir.

Edmund. I shall offend, either to detain or give it. The contents, as in part I understand them, are to blame.

Gloucester. Let's see, let's see.

Edmund. I hope, for my brother's justification, he wrote this but as an essay or taste of my virtue.

Gloucester. 'This policy and reverence of age makes the world bitter to the best of our times; keeps our fortunes from us till our oldness cannot relish them. I begin to find an idle and fond bondage in the oppression of aged tyranny, who sways, not as it hath power, but as it is suffered. Come to me, that of this I may speak more. If our father would sleep till I waked him, you should enjoy half his revenue for ever, and live the beloved of your brother, EDGAR.' — Hum! Conspiracy! 'Sleep till I waked him, you should enjoy half his revenue.'— My son Edgar! Had he a hand to write this? a heart and brain to breed it in? When came this to you? Who brought it?

Edmund. It was not brought me, my lord; there's the cunning of it; I found it thrown in at the casement of

27　So please your lordship: If it please your lordship for me to say so.

28　earnestly: eagerly.　**put up**: put away.

33　terrible: frightened.　**dispatch**: haste in putting away.

37　pardon me: excuse me from showing it you.

38—39　o'er-read: read through.　**for so much as**: as far as.　**o'er-looking**: looking over, reading.

41　to detain or give it: by keeping it back or giving it up.

42　to blame: blameworthy.

45　essay or taste: trial or test.

46　policy and reverence of age: policy of reverence for old age. 伊丽莎白时代英语中 policy 一词常有"狡诈"的含义。此处暗示这种 reverence 是老年人强加于社会的。

47　the best … times: our best days, i.e. men in their prime.

49　idle: wasteful.　**fond**: foolish.

50　aged tyranny: a tyrannical old man, 指其父亲 Gloucester, 这是以抽象代具体。　**sways**: rules.

51　suffered: permitted, tolerated.　**that**: so that.

52—53　sleep till I waked him: i.e. sleep forever, die.　**should**: would.

56—57　revenue: income.　**to write**: in writing.　**breed**: conceive, produce.

60　casement: (open) window.　**closet**: private room.

my closet.

Gloucester. You know the character to be your brother's?

Edmund. If the matter were good, my lord, I durst swear it were his; but, in respect of that, I would fain think it were not.

Gloucester. It is his.

Edmund. It is his hand, my lord; but I hope his heart is not in the contents.

Gloucester. Hath he never heretofore sounded you in this business?

Edmund. Never, my lord; but I have often heard him maintain it to be fit that, sons at perfect age, and fathers declined, the father should be as ward to the son, and the son manage his revenue.

Gloucester. O villain, villain! His very opinion in the letter! Abhorred villain! Unnatural, detested, brutish villain! Worse than brutish! Go, sirrah, seek him; I'll apprehend him. Abomiable villain! Where is he?

Edmund. I do not well know, my lord. If it shall please you to suspend your indignation against my brother till you can derive from him better testimony of his intent, you shall run a certain course; where, if you violently proceed against him, mistaking his purpose, it would make a great gap in your own honour, and shake in pieces the heart of his obedience. I dare pawn down my life for him, that he hath writ this to feel my affection to your honour, and to no other pretence of danger.

Gloucester. Think you so?

Edmund. If your honour judge it meet, I will place you where you shall hear us confer of this, and by an auricular assurance have your satisfaction; and that without any further delay than this very evening.

61 character: hand-writing.
63 matter: subject matter, contents. **durst**: would dare.
64 in respect of: in view of. **that**: the matter.
65 fain: gladly, rather.
69 heretofore: before now. **sounded you**: tried to find out how you feel or think.
72 sons: 后者略 being. **perfect age**: the prime of life, fulll maturity.
73 as ward to: under the guardianship of.
76 Abhorred: abhorrent. **detested**: detestable.
77 sirrah: 父母对儿子或主人对仆人的一种通常称呼。
78 apprehend: seize.
79—80 If…you: If you would kindly agree.
82 run a certain course: act safely. **where**: whereas.
84 gap: breach.
85 shake in pieces: break into pieces.
86 pawn down: stake (in a wager). **writ**: written. 当时的英语允许省去以 en 词尾，又如：chosen-chose, spoken-spoke.
87 feel: try out, test.
87—88 pretence of danger: dangerous intention.
90 meet: fitting.
91—92 confer of: talk about, consult on. **auricular**: through the ear, heard. **satisfaction**: conviction.

Gloucester. He cannot be such a monster—

Edmund. Nor is not, sure.

Gloucester. — to his father, that so tenderly and entirely loves him. Heaven and earth! Edmund, seek him out; wind me into him, I pray you; frame the business after your own wisdom. I would unstate myself to be in a due resolution.

Edmund. I will seek him, sir, presently; convey the business as I shall find means, and acquaint you withal.

Gloucester. These late eclipses in the sun and moon portend no good to us: though the wisdom of nature can reason it thus and thus, yet nature finds itself scourged by the sequent effects. Love cools, friendship falls off, brothers divide: in cities, mutinies; in countries, discord; in palaces, treason; and the bond cracked between son and father. This villain of mine comes under the prediction; there's son against father; the king falls from bias of nature; there's father against child. We have seen the best of our time: machinations, hollowness, treachery, and all ruinous disorders, follow us disquietly to our graves. Find out this villain, Edmund; it shall lose thee nothing: do it carefully. And the noble and true-hearted Kent banished! his offence, honesty! 'Tis strange! [*Exit.*

Edmund. This is the excellent foppery of the world, that, when we are sick in fortune, — often the surfeit of our own behaviour, — we make guilty of our disasters the sun, the moon, and the stars; as if we were villains by necessity, fools by heavenly compulsion, knaves, thieves, and treachers by spherical predominance, drunkards, liars, and adulterers by an enforced obedience of planetary influence; and all that we are evil in, by a divine thrusting on: an admirable evasion

ACT I SCENE II

95 Nor is not：And he is not. 双重否定仍表示否定,但有强调意,这在当时的英语中常见。

96 that：who. **entirely**：whole-heartedly.

98—99 wind me into him：worm your way into his confidence. me 此处不是 wind 的宾语,而是 ethical dative (泛指人称与格) = for me. **frame...after**：manage the affair according to.

99 unstate myself：give up my position.

100 to be...resolution：in order to have my doubts resolved.

101 presently：immediately. **convey**：carry out.

102 acquaint you withal!：inform you of it.

103—104 These...us：莎士比亚时代人普遍认为星象主人世的吉凶。日蚀和月蚀被认为尤其不吉利。 **late**：recent.

104—105 the wisdom...thus and thus：natural philosophy (i.e. science) can give explanations of the occurrence of eclipse.

106 sequent effects：effects that follow (eclipses).

107 mutinies：disturbances.

110 comes...prediction：is one of the predices by ill omens.

111 from bias of nature：away from natural inclination (bias) (i.e. of affection towards Cordelia).

113 machinations：plots. **hollowness**：insincerity.

114 disorders：disorderly practice.

118 foppery：folly.

119 sick in fortune：in trouble. **surfeit**：evil result.

120—121 make guilty...sun：put the blame for our disasters on the sun.

123—124 treachers：traitors. **spherical predominance**：ascendancy of a special star. 中世纪人认为天是一些同心圆球面(spheres),上嵌各类星球。

125 of：to.

126 a divine thrusting on：a supernatural impulse. **admirable**：astonishing. **evasion**：evasion of responsibility.

of whoremaster man, to lay his goatish disposition to the charge of a star! My father compounded with my mother under the dragon's tail, and my nativity was under Ursa Major; so that it follows I am rough and lecherous. 'Sfoot! I should have been that I am had the maidenliest star in the firmament twinkled on my bastardizing. Edgar —

Enter EDGAR.

and pat he comes, like the catastrophe of the old comedy: my cue is villainous melancholy, with a sigh like Tom o'Bedlam. O, these eclipses do portend these divisions! Fa, sol, la, mi.

Edgar. How now, brother Edmund! What serious contemplation are you in?

Edmund. I am thinking, brother, of a prediction I read this other day, what should follow these eclipses.

Edgar. Do you busy yourself with that?

Edmund. I promise you the effects he writes of succeed unhappily; as of unnaturalness between the child and the parent; death, dearth, dissolutions of ancient amities; division in state; menaces and maledictions against king and nobles; needless diffidences, banishment of friends, dissipation of cohorts, nuptial breaches, and I know not what.

Edgar. How long have you been a sectary astronomical?

Edmund. Come, come; when saw you my father last?

Edgar. The night gone by.

Edmund. Spake you with him?

Edgar. Ay, two hours together.

Edmund. Parted you in god terms? Fond you no displeasure in him by word or countenance?

Edgar. None at all.

ACT I SCENE II

127 whoremaster：lecherous.　**goatish**：lustful, lascivious.

128 compounded：copulated.

129 dragon's tail：（月球轨道与黄道的）降交点。

130 Ursa Major：the Great Bear，大熊星座。按星象学的说法，这个星座使人特别淫荡。

131 'Sfoot!：God's foot,呸（表示轻蔑）。　**that**：what.

133 bastardizing：extramarital conception.

134 pat：just at the right moment.　**catastrophe**：戏剧中的结局。

135 cue：part, hint as how to act in this situation.　**villainous**：① extreme；②evil。

136 Tom o' Bedlam：疯乞丐。Bedlam 一词源自伦敦 St. Mary of Bethlehem 医院，收精神病患者。病人出院后流落街头行乞,常常以悲叹引起行人的同情。

137 Fa,…mi：音符。Edmund 哼音乐,假装没听见 Edgar 到来。

141 this other day：the other day.　**what**：as to what.

143 succeed：turn out.

147 diffidences：distrust (of others).

148 dissipation of cohorts：desertion of supporters.

150 sectary astronomical：信奉星象学的人。　**sectary**：believer,形容词在名词后,这是受法语的影响。

151 saw you：did you see.在伊丽莎白时代英语中疑问句可用颠倒主谓的位置构成,而不必加助动词 do (did).

154 two hours together：for a full two hours.

156 countenance：facial expression.

Edmund. Bethink yourself wherein you may have offended him; and at my entreaty forbear his presence
160 till some little time hath qualified the heat of his displeasure, which at this instant so rageth in him that with the mischief of your person it would scarcely allay.

Edgar. Some villain hath done me wrong.

165 *Edmund.* That's my fear. I pray you have a continent forbearance till the speed of his rage goes slower, and, as I say, retire with me to my lodging, from whence I will fitly bring you to hear my lord speak. Pray you, go; there's my key. If you do stir abroad go armed.

170 *Edgar.* Armed, brother!

Edmund. Brother, I advise you to the best; go armed; I am no honest man if there be any good meaning toward you; I have told you what I have seen and heard; but faintly, nothing like the image and horror
175 of it; pray you, away.

Edgar. Shall I hear from you anon?

Edmund. I do serve you in this business.

[*Exit* EDGAR.

A credulous father, and a brother noble,
Whose nature is so far from doing harms
180 That he suspects none; on whose foolish honesty
My practices ride easy! I see the business.
Let me, if not by birth, have lands by wit:
All with me's meet that I can fashion fit. [*Exit*.

158 Bethink yourself wherein: try to think in what way.

159 forbear his presence: avoid meeting him.

160 qualified: reduced, moderated.

162 mischief: injury.

162—163 allay: subside.

165—166 continent forbearance: self-restrained withdrawal (keeping out of his way), cf.I.i 159 行.

168 fitly: at a suitable time. **Pray you**: I beg you.

169 stir abroad: move about away from home.

172 meaning: intention.

174 faintly: euphemistically, 委婉地说。 **image and horror**: horrible reality (image=true likeness).

175 away: 前省略 go.

176 anon: shortly.

181 practices: plots. **I see the business**: I have it all planned (in my mind).

182 wit: cunning.

183 这句话的正常词序为：All that I can fashion fit is meet with me.意思是 Everything that I can contrive to serve my purpose is justified in my eyes.

SCENE III

A ROOM IN THE DUKE OF ALBANY'S PALACE

Enter GONERIL *and* OSWALD *her* Steward.

Goneril. Did my father strike my gentleman for chiding
of his fool?
Oswald. Ay, madam.
Goneril. By day and night he wrongs me; every hour
5 He flashes into one gross crime or other,
That sets us all at odds: I'll not endure it:
His knights grow riotous, and himself upbraids us
On every trifle. When he returns from hunting
I will not speak with him; say I am sick:
10 If you come slack of former services,
You shall do well; the fault of it I'll answer.
Oswald. He's coming, madam; I hear him.

[*Horns within.*

Goneril. Put on what weary negligence you please,
You and your fellows; I'd have it come to question:
15 If he distaste it, let him to my sister,
Whose mind and mine, I know, in that are one,
Not to be over-rul'd. Idle old man,
That still would manage those authorities
That he hath given away! Now, by my life,
20 Old fools are babes again, and must be us'd
With checks as flatteries, when they are seen abus'd.
Remember what I have said.
Oswald.   Well, madam.
Goneril. And let his knights have colder looks among
you;
What grows of it, no matter; advise your fellows so:
25 I would breed from hence occasions, and I shall,

I.iii

    4 **By day and night**: At all times, continually.

    5 **flashes into**: breaks out into.   **crime**: offence, 语义比现代用法轻。

    6 **sets...at odds**: upsets us.

    7 **himself**: he himself. 按当时的语法,反身代词可直接用作主语。

    10 **come...services**: become less diligent in your services to him than before.

    11 **answer**: answer for it, be responsible for it.

    s.d.within: i.e. at the back of the stage. 号角声表示李尔王打猎归来。

    13 **what...you please**: whatever...should please you.

    14 **I'd...question**: I want it (negligence) to be discussed.

    15 **distaste**: dislike.   **let him to**: let him go to. 运动动词 go, come 等在当时的英语中常被省略。

    17 **Idle**: Folish.

    18 **manage those authorities**: exercise the powers.

    20—21 **us'd...abus'd**: treated (used) with rebukes (checks) as well as soothing words (flatteries) when they (the old fools) are seen deluded (misled, abused). 但有的注释者认为 they 指 flatteries, 这样 abused 就应按其本义作"滥用"解。   **as**: as well as, 但也有注释者解为 instead of.

    24 **grows of it**: results from it.   **so**: to the same effect.

    25 **occasions**: opportunities.

That I may speak; I'll write straight to my sister
To hold my very course. Prepare for dinner.

[*Exeunt.*

SCENE IV

A HALL IN THE SAME

Enter KENT, *disguised.*

Kent. If but as well I other accents borrow,
That can my speech defuse, my good intent
May carry through itself to that full issue
For which I raz'd my likeness. Now, banish'd Kent,
If thou canst serve where thou dost stand condemn'd,
So may it come, thy master, whom thou lovest,
Shall find thee full of labours.

Horns within. Enter LEAR, Knights,
and Attendants.

Lear. Let me not stay a jot for dinner; go, get it ready.
[*Exit an* Attendant.] How now! what art thou?

Kent. A man, sir.

Lear. What dost thou profess? What wouldst thou with us?

Kent. I do profess to be no less than I seem; to serve him truly that will put me in trust; to love him that is honest; to converse with him that is wise, and says little; to fear judgment; to fight when I cannot choose; and to eat no fish.

Lear. What art thou?

Kent. A very honest-hearted fellow, and as poor as the king.

Lear. If thou be as poor for a subject as he is for a king, thou art poor enough. What wouldst thou?

ACT I SCENE IV

26 straight：at once.

27 To hold my very course：(telling her) to do exactly as I do.

I. iv

1 此行的正常语序为 If but I borrow other accents as well. **but**：only. **as well**：意即除了化装之外。 **other accents borrow**：take on a different style of speech.

2 defuse：disorder, disguise, make unrecognisable；同 diffuse.

2—3 my good intent…issue：I may be able to bring off my purpose.

4 raz'd my likeness：erased my natural appearance.

5 canst：can 的第二人称单数古体。

6 So…come：有两种解释：①I hope it may come about；②It may so happen (that).

7 full of labours：excellent in service (to the King).

8 stay a jot：wait a moment.

11—12 What…profess?：What is your job? (但下面 Kent 假装把 profess 误解为 claim 的意思。) **What…us?**：What do you want with us? 注意这里省略了动词,这在莎剧中是常见的。

14 put…trust：trust me with his affairs.

15 converse：associate.

16—17 judgment：指上帝和人间的审判,意为敬畏上帝和守法。**when I cannot choose**：when I have no choice.

17 eat no fish：注意解释不一：①是个忠实的新教徒而不是天主教徒,因为天主教家庭有星期五禁肉而吃鱼的习惯,而且当时天主教徒被许多人认为对国家不忠；②非软弱之辈,因为吃肉被认为能使人有力气；③只是为了押头韵(fear-fight-fish)而加上的无足轻重的话。

21 he：i.e. the king, meaning himself.

Kent. Service.

Lear. Whom wouldst thou serve?

Kent. You.

Lear. Dost thou know me, fellow?

Kent. No, sir; but you have that in your countenance which I would fain call master.

Lear. What's that?

Kent. Authority.

Lear. What services canst thou do?

Kent. I can keep honest counsel, ride, run, mar a curious tale in telling it, and deliver a plain message bluntly: that which ordinary men are fit for, I am qualified in, and the best of me is diligence.

Lear. How old art thou?

Kent. Not so young, sir, to love a woman for singing, nor so old to dote on her for any thing; I have years on my back forty-eight.

Lear. Follow me; thou shalt serve me: if I like thee no worse after dinner I will not part from thee yet. Dinner, ho! dinner! Where's my knave? my fool? Go you and call my fool hither. [*Exit an* Attendant.

Enter OSWALD.

You, you, sirrah, where's my daughter?

Oswald. So please you, — [*Exit.*

Lear. What says the fellow there? Call the clotpoll back.

[*Exit* a Knight.] Where's my fool, ho? I think the world's asleep. How now! where's that mongrel?

Re-enter Knight.

Knight. He says, my lord, your daughter is not well.

Lear. Why came not the slave back to me when I called him?

27 countenance: bearing.

32 honest counsel: an honourable secret.　**curious**: elaborate, difficult.

37—38　to love 和 to dote：前均省略 as.

41　yet: for the present.

42　knave: boy, servant, i.e. my fool.

45　So please you: If it pleases you, excuse me (as he goes out).

46　clotpoll: clodpate, blockhead.

48　mongrel：指 Oswald.

Knight. Sir, he answered me in the roundest manner, he would not.

Lear. He would not!

55 *Knight.* My lord, I know not what the matter is; but, to my judgment, your highness is not entertained with that ceremonious affection as you were wont; there's a great abatement of kindness appears as well in the general dependants as in the duke himself also
60 and your daughter.

Lear. Ha! sayest thou so?

Knight. I beseech you, pardon me, my lord, if I be mistaken; for my duty cannot be silent when I think your highness wronged.

65 *Lear.* Thou but rememberest me of mine own conception: I have perceived a most faint neglect of late; which I have rather blamed as mine own jealous curiosity than as a very pretence and purpose of unkindness: I will look further into't. But where's my
70 fool? I have not seen him this two days.

Knight. Since my young lady's going into France, sir, the fool hath much pined him away.

Lear. No more of that; I have noted it well. Go you and tell my daughter I would speak with her.

[*Exit* an Attendant.

75 Go you, call hither my fool.　　[*Exit* an Attendant.

Re-enter OSWALD.

O! you sir, you, come you hither, sir. Whom am I, sir?

Oswald. My lady's father.

Lear. 'My lady's father!' my lord's knave: you whoreson dog! you slave! you cur!

80 *Oswald.* I am none of these, my lord; I beseech your pardon.

52 roundest: plainest, bluntest.
56 entertained: treated.
57 that: such.
59 general dependants: ordinary servants.
61 sayest: say 的古体第二人称单数形式。
63 my duty cannot be: my sense of duty forbids me to be.
65—66 rememberest: remind. **conception**: idea, impression. **faint**: indolent.
67—68 jealous curiosity: over-watchfulness. **very pretence**: real intention.
70 this: these.
72 him: 似乎是多余的,许多版本中无此词。
76 sir: 莎剧中主人称仆人一般用 sirrah,此处反复称 sir 是反话。

Lear. Do you bandy looks with me, you rascal?

[*Striking him.*

Oswald. I'll not be struck, my lord.

Kent. Nor tripped neither, you base football player.

[*Tripping up his heels.*

85 *Lear.* I thank thee, fellow; thou servest me, and I'll love thee.

Kent. Come, sir, arise, away! I'll teach you differences; away, away! If you will measure your lubber's length again, tarry; but away! Go to; have you wisdom? so.

[*Pushes* OSWALD *out.*

90 *Lear.* Now, my friendly knave, I thank thee: there's earnest of thy service. [*Gives* KENT *money.*

Enter Fool.

Fool. Let me hire him too: here's my coxcomb.

[*Offers* KENT *his cap.*

Lear. How now, my pretty knave! how dost thou?

Fool. Sirrah, you were best take my coxcomb.

95 *Kent.* Why, fool?

Fool. Why? for taking one's part that's out of favour. Nay, an thou canst not smile as the wind sits, thou'lt catch cold shortly: there, take my coxcomb. Why, this fellow has banished two on's daughters, and did 100 the third a blessing against his will: if thou follow him thou must needs wear my coxcomb. How now, nuncle! Would I had two coxcombs and two daughters!

Lear. Why, my boy?

Fool. If I gave them all my living, I'd keep my cox-
105 combs myself. There's mine; beg another of thy daughters.

Lear. Take heed, sirrah; the whip.

Fool. Truth's a dog must to kennel; he must be

82　bandy：exchange，网球戏中的回击，仆人是不能平等地回嘴的。

84　football：当时足球是下等人在街头玩的游戏。

87—88　differences：i.e.of rank (between you and a king).

88—89　If…,tarry：If you, you rascal (lubber), want to stretch out your own length (on the ground) again, wait.

89　Go to：away with you（表示厌恶）。　**have you wisdom？**：are you in your senses? **so**：good, that's right.

out：i.e.out of the hall.

91　earnest of：token payment for（付给赏钱）。

92　coxcomb：小丑（弄臣）的帽子，状若鸡冠。

94　you were best：you had better.

96　taking…favour：being on the side of someone who is out of favour.

97　an：if.　**smile as the wind sits**：见风使舵。　**thou'lt**：thou wilt（will 的第二称单数古体）。

99　on's：of his.　**did**：made.

102　nuncle：mine uncle，对主人的一种开玩笑的称呼。　**Would I had**：I wish I had.

104　living：possessions, property.　**keep my coxcombs**：意即我就成了双料小丑了。

107　the whip：这是警告，要鞭打小丑。

108—109　must：that must go. 真理为公狗，不受欢迎，被赶出去，只能待在狗窝里。诺言为母狗，受欢迎，待在室内火炉旁发臭。**brach**：bitch，母狗，显然也指 Goneril 和 Regan 这样的阿谀奉承之辈。

48 KING LEAR

whipped out when Lady the brach may stand by the
fire and stink.

110 *Lear.* A pestilent gall to me!

Fool. [*To* KENT.] Sirrah, I'll teach thee a speech.

Lear. Do.

Fool. Mark it, nuncle: —

    Have more than thou showest,
115   Speak less than thou knowest,
    Lend less than thou owest,
    Ride more than thou goest,
    Learn more than thou trowest,
    Set less than thou throwest;
120   Leave thy drink and thy whore,
      And keep in-a-door,
      And thou shalt have more
      Than two tens to a score.

Kent. This is nothing, fool.

125 *Fool.* Then 'tis like the breath of an unfee'd lawyer, you
gave me nothing for't. Can you make no use of nothing, nuncle?

Lear. Why, no, boy; nothing can be made out of
nothing.

Fool. [*To* KENT.] Prithee, tell him, so much the
130 rent of his land comes to: he will not believe a fool.

Lear. A bitter fool!

Fool. Dost thou know the difference, my boy, between
a bitter fool and a sweet fool?

Lear. No, lad; teach me.

135 *Fool.* That lord that counsell'd thee
    To give away thy land,
   Come place him here by me,
    Do thou for him stand:
   The sweet and bitter fool
140   Will presently appear;

ACT I SCENE IV

110 gall: bitterness.

113 Mark it: Take notice of it. 以下是宫中弄臣的典型的顺口溜,由一组押韵的谚语(有的系即兴编造)构成。

116 owest: own.

117 goest: walk.

118 i.e.(probably) don't believe all you hear. **Learn**: listen. **throwest**: believe, give credit to.

119 i.e. stake less than what you can throw (at a throw of dice).

121 in-a-door: indoors.

122—123 i.e. you'll do well. 这里 score 可能指 20 先令,即一英镑(旧制)。

124 nothing: nonsense.

125 breath: opinion, voice. **an unfee'd lawyer**: a lawyer who has not been paid any fee, and willl therefore not talk on behalf of his client.

130 rent of his land: i.e. nothing, since he has given his land away.

131 bitter: sarcastic.

135 That lord: 指 Lear,但在英国较早的剧本中也有过这样的角色。

138—140 Do…appear: Stand for him (the counsellor), and then the sweet and the bitter fool will be seen at once. 这里 sweet fool 指小丑自己,bitter fool 指 Lear。

> The one in motley here,
>> The other found out there.

Lear. Dost thou call me fool, boy?

Fool. All thy other titles thou hast given away; that thou wast born with.

Kent. This is not altogether fool, my lord.

Fool. No, faith, lords and great men will not let me; if I had a monopoly out, they would have part on't, and ladies too; they will not let me have all fool to myself; they'll be snatching. Nuncle, give me an egg, and I'll give thee two crowns.

Lear. What two crowns shall they be?

Fool. Why, after I have cut the egg i' the middle and eat up the meat, the two crowns of the egg. When thou clovest thy crown i' the middle, and gavest away both parts, thou borest thine ass on thy back o'er the dirt; thou hadst little wit in thy bald crown when thou gavest thy golden one away. If I speak like myself in this, let him be whipped that first finds it so.

> Fools had ne'er less grace in a year;
>> For wise men are grown foppish,
> And know not how their wits to wear,
>> Their manners are so apish.

Lear. When were you wont to be so full of songs, sirrah?

Fool. I have used it, nuncle, ever since thou madest thy daughters thy mothers; for when thou gavest them the rod and puttest down thine own breeches,

> Then they for sudden joy did weep,
>> And I for sorrow sung,
> That such a king should play bo-peep,
>> And go the fools among.

Prithee, nuncle, keep a schoolmaster that can teach thy fool to lie; I would fain learn to lie.

141　**motley**：小丑穿的彩衣。

145　**wast**：be 的第二人称单数过去式古体。

146　**fool**：foolishness.

147　**let me**：i.e.let me be the complete fool.

148　**out**：granted. 英国的国王和女王有时将某种商品的专卖权赐给宠臣，导致该商品的价格昂贵，从而引起公众的极大不满。小丑是说即使自己获得蠢话的专利权，也没法垄断天下的蠢话。这显然是在讽刺时政。　**on't**：on it, i.e.of it.

149—150　**ladies...snatching**：可能暗指抓小丑的形如男性生殖器的手杖。

151　**crowns**：i.e.half shells. 此处又暗指王冠。

154　**eat**：eaten.

155　**clovest**：cleave 的过去式，split in two.

156—157　**borest...dirt**：i.e.reversed the proper order of things. 典出《伊索寓言》。　**borest**：carried.

157　**wit**：good sense.　**crown**：①头顶；②王冠。

158　**like myself**：foolishly.

159　**so**：i.e. foolish. 这句话的意思是：他现在说的不是傻话。如果有人这么认为，那他才该挨鞭子。

160　**Fools...year**：There was never a time when fools were less in favour than now.　**grace**：favour.　**in a year**：in any year, i.e.ever.

161　**foppish**：foolish.

162　**their wits to wear**：show their wisdom.

163　**apish**：spelike, silly.

165　**used it**：made it my habit, made a practice of it.

167　**puttest down**：pulled down.

170　**play bo-peep**：behave like a child. bo-peep 是小孩子玩的躲猫游戏。

172　**Prithee**：I pray you, please.

Lear. An you lie, sirrah, we'll have you whipped.

Fool. I marvel what kin thou and thy daughters are: they'll have me whipped for speaking true, thou'lt have me whipped for lying; and sometimes I am whipped for holding my peace. I had rather be any kind o' thing than a fool; and yet I would not be thee, nuncle; thou hast pared thy wit o'both sides, and left nothing i' the middle: here comes one o' the parings.

Enter GONERIL.

Lear. How now, daughter! what makes that frontlet on?

Methinks you are too much of late i' the frown.

Fool. Thou wast a pretty fellow when thou hadst no need to care for her frowning; now thou art an O without a figure. I am better than thou art now; I am a fool, thou art nothing. [*To* GONERIL.] Yes, forsooth, I will hold my tongue; so your face bids me, though you say nothing.

        Mum, mum;

        He that keeps nor crust nor crumb,

        Weary of all, shall want some.

That's a shealed peascod.   [*Pointing to* LEAR.

Goneril. Not only, sir, this your all-licens'd fool,
But other of your insolent retinue
Do hourly carp and quarrel, breaking forth
In rank and not-to-be-endured riots. Sir,
I had thought, by making this well known unto you,
To have found a safe redress; but now grow fearful,
By what yourself too late have spoke and done,
That you protect this course, and put it on
By your allowance; which if you should, the fault
Would not 'scape censure, nor the redresses sleep,
Which, in the tender of a wholesome weal,

174 An: If.

178 holding my peace: remaining silent.

180—181 pared…middle: i. e. by giving away both halves of your kingdom.

182 makes: means. **frontlet**: i. e. frown, 本义为围在额头的额带。

183 Methinks: It seems to me.

184 pretty: fine.

185 care for: worry about.

185—186 an O…figure: a zero without any digit in front of it.

187—188 forsooth: indeed.

190 Mum: Not a word!

191—192 He…some: i. e. He who gives everything away because he's tired of it will later need some part of what he has lost. **crumb**: 是面包心，crust 是面包皮，加在一起就是整个面包。

192 want: need.

193 shealed peascod: shelled peapod, i. e. shell without peas.

194 all-licens'd: privileged to do or say anything he likes.

195 other: others.

196 carp: find fault, prate.

197 rank: gross, coarse.

199 safe redress: sure remedy. **fearful**: afraid.

200 too late: just now, all too recently.

201 put it on: encourage it.

202 allowance: approval, permission.

202—207 which…proceeding: and if you do this, I will censure you for it (not 'scape censure), and in order to put things right, it will be necessary to take active measures (redresses) which, in our earnest desire (tender) for a healthy state (wholesome weal), may offend you in the way they work out and would otherwise be thought shameful (which else were shame), but which the needs of the situation show to be acts of good sense (discreet proceeding). Goneril 在这里故意咬文嚼字，避免用第一人称并使用晦涩难懂、结构复杂的长句，以免与 Lear 发生正面冲突。注意这里用的三个 which 和一个 that 都是引出定语从句的关系代词。其中第一个 which (202 行) 指上文的 protect this course, and put it on by your allowance, 另外两个 which 和 that 都指 redresses。

205 Might in their working do you that offence,
Which else were shame, that then necessity
Will call discreet proceeding.
Fool. For you trow, nuncle,
The hedge-sparrow fed the cuckoo so long,
210 That it had it head bit off by it young.
So out went the candle, and we were left darkling.
Lear. Are you our daughter?
Goneril. I would you would make use of your good wisdom,
Whereof I know you are fraught; and put away
215 These dispositions which of late transform you
From what you rightly are.
Fool. May not an ass know when the cart draws the horse? Whoop, Jug! I love thee.
Lear. Does any here know me? This is not Lear:
220 Does Lear walk thus? speak thus? Where are his eyes?
Either his notion weakens, his discernings
Are lethargied. Ha! waking? 'tis not so.
Who is it that can tell me who I am?
Fool. Lear's shadow.
225 *Lear.* I would learn that; for, by the marks of sovereignty, knowledge and reason, I should be false persuaded I had daughters.
Fool. Which they will make an obedient father.
Lear. Your name, fair gentlewoman?
230 *Goneril.* This admiration, sir, is much o' the favour
Of other your new pranks. I do beseech you
To understand my purposes aright:
As you are old and reverend, should be wise.
Here do you keep a hundred knights and squires;
235 Men so disorder'd, so debosh'd, and bold,
That this our court, infected with their manners,

ACT I SCENE IV

208 trow: know.

210 后两个 it＝its,中世纪 it 的所有格不变。这两行是押韵对句,可能出自谚语:布谷鸟把蛋下在篱雀的窝里。篱雀代为孵卵并把小鸟喂大。但小布谷鸟长大以后个子很大,却把别的蛋和雏鸟都推出窝外并把养育它的篱雀的头咬掉。

211 darkling: in the dark.

214 fraught: stored, amply provided.

215 dispositions: moods.

217—218 May … horse?: Can't even a fool see when the cart is pulling the horse? 意思是:现在当女儿的却在向父亲发号施令,这不明明是是非颠倒吗? cf.(谚语) to put the cart before the horse.

218 Whoop,Jug!: 出处不详。一说可能是赶车时吆喝牲口的声音。一说可能源自久已失传的一首古老的歌曲。

221 notion: understanding. **discernings**: powers of discernment.

222 lethargied: dulled. **waking?**: am I awake?

225 I would: I must. **learn**: find out.

226 false: falsely.

228 Which: Whom,指 Lear's shadow 或 I.

230 admiration: feigned surprise. **favour**: nature.

231 other your: your other.

235 disorder'd: disorderly. **debosh'd**: debauched.

Shows like a riotous inn: epicurism and lust
Make it more like a tavern or a brothel
Than a grac'd palace. The shame itself doth speak
For instant remedy; be then desir'd
By her that else will take the thing she begs,
A little to disquantity your train;
And the remainder, that shall still depend,
To be such men as may besort your age,
Which know themselves and you.
Lear.   Darkness and devils!
Saddle my horses; call my train together.
Degenerate bastard! I'll not trouble thee:
Yet have I left a daughter.
Goneril. You strike my people, and your disorder'd rabble
Make servants of their betters.

Enter ALBANY.

Lear. Woe, that too late repents;
           [*To* ALBANY.] O! sir, are you come?
Is it your will? Speak, sir. Prepare my horses.
Ingratitude, thou marble-hearted fiend,
More hideous, when thou show'st thee in a child,
Than the sea-monster.
Albany.   Pray, sir, be patient.
Lear. [*To* GONERIL.] Detested kite! thou liest:
My train are men of choice and rarest parts,
That all particulars of duty know,
And in the most exact regard support
The worships of their name. O most small fault,
How ugly didst thou in Cordelia show!
Which, like an engine, wrench'd my frame of nature
From the fix'd place, drew from my heart all love,
And added to the gall. O Lear, Lear, Lear!

237 Shows: Looks. **epicurism**: epicureanism, luxury.

239 grac'd: honourable.

239—240 speak/For: demand.

240 be then desir'd: let yourself be requested.

241 that else: who otherwise.

242 disquantity your train: reduce the number of your attendants.

243—244 the remainder, .../To be: allow the remainder to be. **depend**: serve you

244 besort: suit, befit.

245 Which: Who.

246 train: attendants.

248 left a daughter: one daughter left, i. e. Regan.

251 Woe, that: Woe to him who. **are you come?**: have you come.

252 Is it you will?: Is this what you wan?

254 thou show'st thee: you show yourself.

255 the: a (generic use).

256 kite (fig.): rapacious person.

257 choice and rarest parts: the choicest and rarest qualities. 当时的英语允许两个形容词共用一个最高级词尾。

258 That...know: Who know their duty down to the smallest detail.

259—260 And...name: And live up to their reputation (worships of their name) with greatest care (in the most exact regard). **worships**: 在当时的英语中，抽象名词在指多人时可用复数。

260 O...fault: i. e. Cordelia's obstinacy.

262—263 Which, ... place: Which, like a rack (engine), wrenched my natural frame (frame of nature) out of its proper shape (from the fixed place).

264 gall: 胆汁, bitterness.

265 Beat at this gate, that let thy folly in,
[*Striking his head.*
And thy dear judgment out! Go, go, my people.
Albany. My lord, I am guiltless, as I am ignorant
Of what hath mov'd you.
Lear. It may be so, my lord.
Hear, Nature, hear! dear goddess, hear!
270 Suspend thy purpose, if thou didst intend
To make this creature fruitful!
Into her womb convey sterility!
Dry up in her the organs of increase,
And from her derogate body never spring
275 A babe to honour her! If she must teem,
Create her child of spleen, that it may live
And be a thwart disnatur'd torment to her!
Let it stamp wrinkles in her brow of youth,
With cadent tears fret channels in her cheeks,
280 Turn all her mother's pains and benefits
To laughter and contempt, that she may feel
How sharper than a serpent's tooth it is
To have a thankless child! Away, away! [*Exit.*
Albany. Now, gods that we adore, whereof comes this?
285 *Goneril.* Never afflict yourself to know the cause;
But let his disposition have that scope
That dotage gives it.

Re-enter LEAR.

Lear. What! fifty of my followers at a clap,
Within a fortnight?
Albany. What's the matter, sir?
290 *Lear.* I'll tell thee. [*To* GONERIL.] Life and death! I am asham'd
That thou hast power to shake my manhood thus,

ACT I SCENE IV

266 dear: precious.
268 mov'd: agitated, angered.
274 derogate: debased, degraded.
275 teem: bear children.
276 spleen: malice, spitefulness. 古人认为脾主怒和恨。 **that**: so that. **it**: 指 child, 278 行同。
277 thwart: cross, perverse. **disnatur'd**: unnatural, unfilial.
278 brow of youth: youthful brow.
279 cadent: falling. **fret**: wear away.
280 mother's: maternal. **benefits**: kindnesses shown to the child.
281 laughter: mockery.
285 afflict: worry, trouble.
286 disposition: mood.
288 at a clap: at a stroke, all at once.
290 Life and death!: By life and death(一种赌咒语)。

That these hot tears, which break from me perforce,
Should make thee worth them. Blasts and fogs upon thee!
Th' untented woundings of a father's curse
295 Pierce every sense about thee! Old fond eyes,
Beweep this cause again, I'll pluck ye out,
And cast you, with the waters that you lose,
To temper clay. Yes, is it come to this?
Let it be so: I have another daughter,
300 Who, I am sure, is kind and comfortable:
When she shall hear this of thee, with her nails
She'll flay thy wolvish visage. Thou shalt find
That I'll resume the shape which thou dost think
I have cast off for ever; thou shalt, I warrant thee.
  [*Exeunt* LEAR, KENT, *and* Attendants.
305 *Goneril*. Do you mark that?
 Albany. I cannot be so partial, Goneril,
  To the great love I bear you. —
 Goneril. Pray you, content. What, Oswald, ho!
  [*To* the Fool.] You, sir, more knave than fool, after your master.
310 *Fool*. Nuncle Lear, nuncle Lear! tarry, and take the fool with thee.

      A fox, when one has caught her,
      And such a daughter,
      Should sure to the slaughter,
315   If my cap would buy a halter;
      So the fool follows after. [*Exit*.

 Goneril. This man hath had good counsel. A hundred knights!
  'Tis politic and safe to let him keep
  At point a hundred knights; yes, that on every dream,
320 Each buzz, each fancy, each complaint, dislike,

ACT I SCENE IV

292 perforce: against one's will.

293 Blasts: blights.　**fogs**: 当时的人认为雾传染疾病。

294 untented: too deep to be probed and cleaned. tent 原意为外科医生用以探测或清洗伤口的棉花塞条,用作动词时意为用塞条探测或清洗。

295 fond: foolish.

296 Beweep: (If you) weep over.

297 lose: waste.

298 temper: moisten.

300 comfortable: comforting, ready to offer comfort.

303 shape: authority.

305 mark: notice.

306—307 i. e. so prejudiced by (partial to) my love for you (as to approve your conduct now).

308 (be) **content**: 别说了。

309 after: go after, follow.

314 Should sure: Should surely go.

317 This man: 指 Lear. 下面的话全是反话。　**counsel**: advice.

318 politic: in accordance with good policy, prudent.

319 At point: Armed and ready.

320 buzz: rumour.

He may enguard his dotage with their powers,
And hold our lives in mercy. Oswald, I say!
Albany. Well, you may fear too far.
Goneril. Safer than trust too far.
Let me still take away the harms I fear,
325 Not fear still to be taken: I know his heart.
What he hath utter'd I have writ my sister;
If she sustain him and his hundred knights,
When I have show'd the unfitness, —

Re-enter OSWALD.

How now, Oswald!
What! have you writ that letter to my sister?
330 *Oswald.* Ay, madam.
Goneril. Take you some company, and away to horse:
Inform her full of my particular fear;
And thereto add such reasons of your own
As may compact it more. Get you gone,
335 And hasten your return.[*Exit* OSWALD.] No, no, my lord,
This milky gentleness and course of yours
Though I condemn not, yet, under pardon,
You are much more attask'd for want of wisdom
Than prais'd for harmful mildness.
340 *Albany.* How far your eyes may pierce I cannot tell:
Striving to better, oft we mar what's well.
Goneril. Nay, then —
Albany. Well, well; the event. [*Exeunt.*

SCENE V

COURT BEFORE THE SAME
Enter LEAR, KENT, *and* FOOL.

Lear. Go you before to Gloucester with these letters.
Acquaint my daughter no further with any thing you

321　enguard: guard, protect.

322　in mercy: at his mercy.

324　still: always.

325　Not...taken: Not always be in fear of being overtaken (taken) by harm.

326　writ: written. (I.i 329 行同)

327　sustain: maintain.

329　What!: Well!

332　full: fully, in full.　**particular**: personal.

334　compact: strengthen, confirm.

336　milky: mild.　**gentleness and course**: gentle course of action. 用一个抽象名词加另一个名词代替一个形容词加名词的修辞手法，叫重言法(hendiadys)。

337　under pardon: if you will forgive me for saying so.

338　attask'd: blamed, held to account (from tasked).

339　harmful mildness: a mildness which can only prove harmful to us.

343　the event: let us see what turns out.

I.v

1　Gloucester: 这里指地方而非指人。　**these letters**: this letter.

know than comes from her demand out of the letter. If your diligence be not speedy I shall be there before you.

Kent. I will not sleep, my lord, till I have delivered your letter. [*Exit.*

Fool. If a man's brains were in 's heels, were't not in danger of kibes?

Lear. Ay, boy.

Fool. Then, I prithee, be merry; thy wit shall not go slip-shod.

Lear. Ha, ha, ha!

Fool. Shalt see thy other daughter will use thee kindly; for though she's as like this as a crab is like an apple, yet I can tell what I can tell.

Lear. What canst tell, boy?

Fool. She will taste as like this as a crab does to a crab. Thou canst tell why one's nose stands i' the middle on's face?

Lear. No.

Fool. Why, to keep one's eyes of either side's nose, that what a man cannot smell out, he may spy into.

Lear. I did her wrong, —

Fool. Canst tell how an oyster makes his shell?

Lear. No.

Fool. Nor I either; but I can tell why a snail has a house.

Lear. Why?

Fool. Why, to put his head in; not to give it away to his daughters, and leave his horns without a case.

Lear. I will forget my nature. So kind a father! Be my horses ready?

Fool. Thy asses are gone about 'em. The reason why the seven stars are no more than seven is a pretty reason.

ACT I SCENE V

3 demand out of: questions arising from.

4 If…speedy: If you do not travel quickly. **diligence**: despatch, speed.

7 's: his. **'t**: it, 指 his brain(s).

8 kibes: chilblains, 冻疮。

11 slip-shod: in slippers (to ease chilblains on the heels). 这句话的意思是：You will never have to wear slippers because of chilbrains, for you show you have no wit, even in your heels, in undertaking your journey to Regan.

13 kindly: 双关语 1. affectionately; 2. according to her true nature.

14 this: this one, i. e. Goneril. **crab**: crab apple, 沙果（状似苹果而小，味酸）。

18 on's: of one's.

20 of: on. **'s nose**: of one's nose.

21 spy: look closely.

28 horns: 触角。 **case**: covering, 壳。

29 my nature: my natural affection (for my daughters). **kind**: 参见 13 行。

31 asses: idiots (who still serve you). **about 'em**: to see about them.

32 the seven stars: the Pleiades, 昴星团, 其中七颗肉眼可见。 **pretty**: apt.

Lear. Because they are not eight?

Fool. Yes, indeed; thou wouldst make a good fool.

35 *Lear.* To take it again perforce! Monster ingratitude!

Fool. If thou wert my fool, nuncle, I'd have thee beaten for being old before thy time.

Lear. How's that?

Fool. Thou shouldst not have been old before thou
40 hadst been wise.

Lear. O! let me not be mad, not mad, sweet heaven;
Keep me in temper; I would not be mad!

Enter Gentleman.

How now! Are the horses ready?

Gentleman. Ready, my lord.

45 *Lear.* Come, boy.

Fool. She that's a maid now, and laughs at my departure,

Shall not be a maid long, unless things be cut shorter.
[*Exeunt.*

ACT I SCENE V

35 To take…perforce!：To take it back (again) by force. Lear 此话可作两种理解：①Lear 可能在想用武力夺回王权；②Lear 在想 Goneril 剥夺他的特权一事。

42 temper：mental balance, normal state of mind.

46—47 这个押韵对句是对观众说的旁白。意思是说，在座的女郎如果只觉得小丑的话滑稽而没有看到即将来临的不幸，她的头脑就简单得恐怕连自己的贞操都保不住了。　**departure**：①下场；②文字游戏。按当时的发音这个词与 shorter 押韵。　**things**：penises.

ACT II

SCENE I

A COURT WITHIN THE CASTLE OF
THE EARL OF GLOUCESTER

Enter EDMUND *and* CURAN, *meeting*.

Edmund. Save thee, Curan.
Curan. And you, sir. I have been with your father, and given him notice that the Duke of Cornwall and Regan his duchess will be here with him to-night.
5 *Edmund.* How comes that?
Curan. Nay, I know not. You have heard of the news abroad? I mean the whispered ones, for they are yet but ear-kissing arguments?
Edmund. Not I: pray you, what are they?
10 *Curan.* Have you heard of no likely wars toward, 'twixt the Dukes of Cornwall and Albany?
Edmund. Not a word.
Curan. You may do then, in time. Fare you well, sir.
[*Exit.*
Edmund. The duke be here to-night! The better! best!
15   This weaves itself perforce into my business.

Enter EDGAR

    My father hath set guard to take my brother;
    And I have one thing, of a queasy question,
    Which I must act. Briefness and fortune, work!
    Brother, a word; descend: brother, I say!
20   My father watches: O sir! fly this place;
    Intelligence is given where you are hid;
    You have now the good advantage of the night.
    Have you not spoken 'gainst the Duke of Cornwall?
    He's coming hither, now, i' the night, i' the haste,

ACT II SCENE I

II.i

1　Save thee：May God save thee 的缩略形式，问候语。

2　And you：May God save you, too. Edmund 称 Curan "thee"，态度高傲；Curan 称 Edmund "you, Sir"，态度谦恭。

6－7　news abroad：rumours going about，在后文中 news 被当作复数，与现代英语用法不同。

7　ones：news.

8　ear-kissing arguments：subjects of whispered conversation.

10　toward：in view, about to take place，修饰 wars.

14　be：will be.　**The better!**：So much the better!

15　weaves：fits, dovetails.　**perforce**：necessarily.

16　set guard：sent out guards.　**take**：seize, capture.

17　queasy question：ticklish problem.

18　act：do.　**Briefness**：speed, prompt action.

19　descend：Edgar 大概从舞台后部楼梯下来。

20　fly：flee.

21　Intelligence is given：It is known (through secret informers). **hid**：hidden.

24　i' the haste：in haste.

25 And Regan with him; have you nothing said
Upon his party 'gainst the Duke of Albany?
Advise yourself.
Edgar.   I am sure on't, not a word.
Edmund. I hear my father coming; pardon me;
In cunning I must draw my sword upon you;
30 Draw; seem to defend yourself; now 'quit you well.
Yield; — come before my father. Light, ho! here!
Fly, brother. Torches! torches! So, farewell.
                              [*Exit* EDGAR.
Some blood drawn on me would beget opinion
                              [*Wounds his arm.*
Of my more fierce endeavour: I have seen drunkards
35 Do more than this in sport. Father! father!
Stop, stop! No help?

Enter GLOUCESTER, *and* Servants *with torches.*

Gloucester. Now, Edmund, where's the villain?
Edmund. Here stood he in the dark, his sharp sword out,
Mumbling of wicked charms, conjuring the moon
40 To stand auspicious mistress.
Gloucester.   But where is he?
Edmund. Look, sir, I bleed.
Gloucester.   Where is the villain, Edmund?
Edmund. Fled this way, sir. When by no means he could—
Gloucester. Pursue him, ho! Go after. [*Exeunt some*
Servants.] 'By no means' what?
Edmund. Persuade me to the murder of your lordship;
45 But that I told him, the revenging goods
'Gainst parricides did all their thunders bend;
Spoke with how manifold and strong a bond
The child was bound to the father; sir, in fine,
Seeing how loathly opposite I stood
50 To his unnatural purpose, in fell motion,

26 Upon his party 'gainst: For his side (case, part) against.
27 Advise yourself: Think carefully. **on't**: of it.
29 In cunning: In crafty pretence.
30 'quit you well: acquit yourself well in action, defend yourself well.
31 Yield: 这话是大声说给 Gloucester 听的。
33—34 beget … endeavour: gain the reputation that I have been fighting more fiercely.
39 Mumbling of: Mumbling, a-mumbling of.
40 stand auspicious mistress: act in the capacity of his fortune-bringing mistress.
44 Persuade me to: Urge me to carry out.
45 But that …：这段话句子结构松散，语法关系不清。前面42行开始的 when clause 没有主句，But that (=But) 又开始了一个新句子；47行的 Spoke 前面还少一个 and。Edmund 故意说话断断续续，以示情急慌乱。
47 with：短语修饰下行 was bound。
48 in fine: in the end.
49 loathly opposite: opposed with loathing.
50 fell motion: a fierce thrust. motion 是击剑术语。

With his prepared sword he charges home
My unprovided body, lanc'd mine arm:
But when he saw my best alarum'd spirits
Bold in the quarrel's right, rous'd to the encounter,
55 Or whether gasted by the noise I made,
Full suddenly he fled.
Gloucester. Let him fly far:
Not in this land shall he remain uncaught;
And found — dispatch. The noble duke my master,
My worthy arch and patron, comes to-night:
60 By his authority I will proclaim it,
That he which finds him shall deserve our thanks,
Bringing the murderous coward to the stake;
He that conceals him, death.
Edmund. When I dissuaded him from his intent,
65 And found him pight to do it, with curst speech
I threaten'd to discover him: he replied,
'Thou unpossessing bastard! dost thou think,
If I would stand against thee, would the reposal
Of any trust, virtue, or worth, in thee
70 Make thy words faith'd? No: what I should deny, —
As this I would; ay, though thou didst produce
My very character, — I'd turn it all
To thy suggestion, plot, and damned practice:
And thou must make a dullard of the world,
75 If they not thought the profits of my death
Were very pregnant and potential spurs
To make thee seek it.'
Gloucester. Strong and fasten'd villain!
Would he deny his letter? I never got him.

[*Tucket within.*

Hark! the duke's trumpets. I know not why he comes.
80 All ports I'll bar; the villain shall not 'scape;
The duke must grant me that: besides, his picture

ACT II SCENE I   73

   52   **unprovided**: unarmed. **lanc'd**: pierced.
   53   **best alarum'd**: fully roused.
   54   **in the quarrel's right**: in support of my complaint.
   55   **gasted**: made aghast, frightened.
   58   **found—dispatch**: when he is found, kill him.
   59   **arch and patron**: principal patron, 指 Cornwall.
   61   **he which**: he who, whoever.
   62   **the stake**: 火刑柱。
   63   **death**: 前省略 shall deserve.
   65   **pight**: pitched, determined. **curst**: cursed, angry, harsh.
   66   **discover**: expose, unmask.
   67   **unpossessing**: unable to inherit.
   68   **would**: should. **stand against**: testify against (e.g. at court). **reposal**: placing.
   70   **faith'd**: believed.
   71   **though**: even though.
   72   **character**: handwriting, i. e. letter.
   73   **suggestion**: prompting to evil. **practice**: treachery.
   74   **make...world**: suppose people very stupid.
   75   **not thought**: should not think. **of**: resulting from.
   76   **pregnant and potential**: obvious and powerful. **spurs**: incentives.
   77   **it**: i. e. my death. **fasten'd**: confirmed, hardened.
   78   **got**: begot.
   Tucket within: a trumpet played offstage.
   80   **ports**: gates. **'scape**: escape.

I will send far and near, that all the kingdom
May have due note of him; and of my land,
Loyal and natural boy, I'll work the means
To make thee capable.

Enter CORNWALL, REGAN, *and* Attendants.

Cornwall. How now, my noble friend! since I came hither, —
   Which I can call but now, — I have heard strange news.
Regan. If it be true, all vengeance comes too short
   Which can pursue the offender. How dost, my lord?
Gloucester. O! madam, my old heart is crack'd, it's crack'd.
Regan. What! did my father's godson seek your life?
   He whom my father nam'd? your Edgar?
Gloucester. O! lady, lady, shame would have it hid.
Regan. Was he not companion with the riotous knights
   That tend upon my father?
Gloucester. I know not, madam; 'tis too bad, too bad.
Edmund. Yes, madam, he was of that consort.
Regan. No marvel then though he were ill affected;
   'Tis they have put him on the old man's death,
   To have the expense and waste of his revenues.
   I have this present evening from my sister
   Been well-inform'd of them, and with such cautions
   That if they come to sojourn at my house,
   I'll not be there.
Cornwall.   Nor I, assure thee, Regan.
   Edmund. I hear that you have shown your father
   A child-like office.
Edmund.   'Twas my duty, sir.
Gloucester. He did bewray his practice; and receiv'd
   This hurt you see, striving to apprehend him.
Cornwall. Is he pursu'd?
Gloucester.   Ay, my good lord.

84   natural：①true，affectionate；②bastard.

85   capable：legally able to inherit (cf.1.67).capable 下接 83 行的 of my land.

89   How dost：How do you do. dost 是 do 的第二人称单数现在时形式。

92   nam'd：i. e. in baptism. 教父在孩子受洗礼时给他命名。

93   hid：hiddden.

97   consort：company.重音在第二音节上。

98   No marvel … affected：It is not surprising if he was intent on evil.

99   they：后面省略 who.   **put him on**：urged on him.

100   to have … waste of：in order to be able to spend his income wastefully.

102   of them：about the riotous knights.

104   assure thee：前面省略 I.

106   child-like：truly filial.   **office**：service.

107   bewray：reveal.   **his**：Edgar's.   **practice**：plot.

108   apprehend：seize.

110 *Cornwall.* If he be taken he shall never more
Be fear'd of doing harm; make your own purpose,
How in my strength you please. For you, Edmund,
Whose virtue and obedience doth this instant
So much commend itself, you shall be ours:
115 Natures of such deep trust we shall much need;
You we first seize on.
Edmund. I shall serve you, sir,
Truly, however else.
Gloucester. For him I thank your Grace.
Cornwall. You know not why we came to visit you,—
Regan. Thus out of season, threading dark-ey'd night:
120 Occasions, noble Gloucester, of some prize,
Wherein we must have use of your advice.
Our father he hath writ, so hath our sister,
Of differences, which I best thought it fit
To answer from our home; the several messengers
125 From hence attend dispatch. Our good old friend,
Lay comforts to your bosom, and bestow
Your needful counsel to our businesses,
Which craves the instant use.
Gloucester. I serve you, madam.
Your Graces are right welcome. [*Exeunt.*

SCENE II

BEFORE GLOUCESTER'S CASTLE

Enter KENT *and* OSWALD, *severally.*

Oswald. Good dawning to thee, friend: art of this house?
Kent. Ay.
Oswald. Where may we set our horses?
Kent. I' the mire.
5 *Oswald.* Prithee, if thou lovest me, tell me.
Kent. I love thee not.
Oswald. Why, then I care not for thee.

ACT II SCENE II

111 of doing: lest he should do.

111—112 make…please: decide on your own purpose as you like so long as it is within my authority.

112 For: As for.

113 virtue and obedience: virtuous obedience,所以用单数动词。

117 however else: however else it may be, whatever may happen.

119 threading dark-ey'd night: making our way with difficulty through the darkness,这个暗喻含义双关语 1. the dark eyes of night; 2. the eye of a needle.

120 Occasions…prize: Occurrences of some importance.此句无动词。

122 writ: written.

123 differences: quarrels. **which**: i. e. in a letter which.

124 from: away from.

125 attend dispatch: wait to be sent out.

126 Lay…bosom: Be consoled.

127 needful counsel to: counsel which is needful to.

128 craves…use: requires immediate attention.

129 right: very.

II.ii

s.d. *severally*: separately, i. e. from different directions.

1 art of this house?: are you of this house? do you belong (as a servant) to this house?

3 set: tie up, stable.

Kent. If I had thee in Lipsbury pinfold, I would make thee care for me.

Oswald. Why dost thou use me thus? I know thee not.

Kent. Fellow, I know thee.

Oswald. What dost thou know me for?

Kent. A knave, a rascal, an eater of broken meats; a base, proud, shallow, beggarly, three-suited, hundred-pound, filthy, worsted-stocking knave; a lily-liver'd, action-taking knave; a whoreson, glass-gazing, superserviceable, finical rogue; one-trunk-inheriting slave; one that wouldst be a bawd, in way of good service, and art nothing but the composition of a knave, beggar, coward, pandar, and the son and heir of a mongrel bitch: one whom I will beat into clamorous whining if thou deniest the least syllable of thy addition.

Oswald. Why, what a monstrous fellow art thou, thus to rail on one that is neither known of thee nor knows thee!

Kent. What a brazen-faced varlet art thou, to deny thou knowest me! Is it two days since I tripped up thy heels and beat thee before the king? Draw, you rogue; for, though it be night, yet the moon shines: I'll make a sop o' the moonshine of you. [*Drawing his sword.*] Draw, you whoreson, cullionly, barber-monger, draw.

Oswald. Away! I have nothing to do with thee.

Kent. Draw, you rascal; you come with letters against the king, and take Vanity the puppet's part against the royalty of her father. Draw, you rogue, or I'll so carbonado your shanks: draw, you rascal; come your ways.

Oswald. Help, ho! murder! help!

Kent. Strike, you slave; stand, rogue, stand; you neat slave, strike. [*Beating him.*

Oswald. Help, oh! murder! murder!

8　in Lipsbury pinfold：当时是否真有一个叫 Lipsbury 的牲畜栏，现已不可考。有人认为这是戏谑语，意为'between my lips'，也就是'in my power'的意思。

10　use：treat.

12　for：as.

13　broken meats：scraps of food from a master's table.

14　three-suited：仆人一年发三套号衣。　**hundred-pound**：妄想当绅士的人。当时至少要有一百镑家当才能称得上'gentleman'.

15—16　worsted：woollen.当时上流社会时尚穿丝袜。穿羊毛袜子被人瞧不起。　**lily-liver'd**：cowardly.

16—17　action-taking：resorting to legal protection (instead of defending oneself).　**glass-gazing**：总是照镜子自我欣赏的。　**super-serviceable**：over-ready to serve people of higher rank.

17　finical：finicky, overfastidious.　**one-trunk-inheriting**：owning only one trunkful of possessions.

18　in way of：in order to perform, as regards.

19　composition：mixture.

20　pandar：pander 的异体字，拉皮条者。

22　thy addition：the names I have just given you.

24　of thee：to you.

27　Draw：Draw your sword.

29　sop…moonshine：①mess；②杀掉 Oswald，让他陈尸在月光之下，像面包吸水那样吸收月光。

30　cullionly：rascally.　**barber-monger**：frequenter of barber's shop, fop.

33　Vanity the puppet：中世纪木偶戏道德剧中的 Vanity（虚荣心）这一角色，此处指 Goneril。

35　carbonado：slash.　**come your ways**：come on.

37　neat：dandified, foppish.

Enter EDMUND, *with his rapier drawn.*

40 *Edmund.* How now! What's the matter?

[*Parting them.*

Kent. With you, goodman boy, if you please: come, I'll flesh ye; come on, young master.

Enter CORNWALL, REGAN, GLOUCESTER, *and* Servants.

Gloucester. Weapons! arms! What's the matter here?
Cornwall. Keep peace, upon your lives:
45 He dies that strikes again. What is the matter?
Regan. The messengers from our sister and the king.
Cornwall. What is your difference? speak.
Oswald. I am scarce in breath, my lord.
Kent. No marvel, you have so bestirred your valour.
50 You cowardly rascal, nature disclaims in thee: a tailor made thee.
Cornwall. Thou art a strange fellow; a tailor make a man?
Kent. Ay, a tailor, sir: a stone-cutter or a painter
55 could not have made him so ill, though they had been but two hours o' the trade.
Cornwall. Speak yet, how grew your quarrel?
Oswald. This ancient ruffian, sir, whose life I have spar'd at suit of his grey beard, —
60 *Kent.* Thou whoreson zed! thou unnecessary letter! My lord, if you will give me leave, I will tread this unbolted villain into mortar, and daub the wall of a jakes with him. Spare my grey beard, you wagtail?
Cornwall. Peace, sirrah!
65 You beastly knave, know you no reverence?
Kent. Yes, sir; but anger hath a privilege.
Cornwall. Why art thou angry?
Kent. That such a slave as this should wear a sword,

ACT II SCENE II

40　matter: subject of the quarrel.

Parting: Separating, disengaging.

41　With you: i.e. The quarrel is with you.　**goodman boy**: 对 Edmund 带有嘲弄口吻的尊称。

42　flesh: initiate (into bloodshed). 原为狩猎用语,意思是在训练猎狗或猎鹰时喂以猎物的肉,使之更为凶猛。也有人解作 cut into your flesh.

44　upon your lives: at the risk of losing your lives.

47　difference: (ground of) quarrel.

49　bestirred: stirred up, used.

50　disclaims in thee: disowns you, renounces any claim to have produced you.

50—51　a tailor made thee: cf. the proverb: "The tailor makes the man."

54　stone-cutter: sculptor.

55　ill: badly.

58　ancient: old.

59　at suit of: at the plea of.

60　zed: 英语字母表中最后一个字母 Z 在莎士比亚时代的词典中常被略去,认为是多余的。

61　leave: permission.　**unbolted**: unsifted, coarse.

63　jakes: privy.　**wagtail**: 鹡鸰鸟,行走时头部和尾巴不住地上下颠动。此处用以形容 Oswald 奴颜婢膝的丑态。

Who wears no honesty. Such smiling rogues as these,
70 Like rats, oft bite the holy cords a-twain
Which are too intrinse t' unloose; smooth every passion
That in the natures of their lords rebel;
Bring oil to fire, snow to their colder moods,
Renege, affirm, and turn their halcyon beaks
75 With every gale and vary of their masters,
Knowing nought, like dogs, but following.
A plague upon your epileptic visage!
Smile you my speeches, as I were a fool?
Goose, if I had you upon Sarum plain,
80 I'd drive ye cackling home to Camelot.
Cornwall. What! art thou mad, old fellow?
Gloucester. How fell you out? say that.
Kent. No contraries hold more antipathy
Than I and such a knave.
85 *Cornwall.* Why dost thou call him knave? What is his fault?
Kent. His countenance likes me not.
Cornwall. No more, perchance, does mine, nor his, nor hers.
Kent. Sir, 'tis my occupation to be plain:
I have seen better faces in my time
90 Than stands on any shoulder than I see
Before me at this instant.
Cornwall.   This is some fellow,
Who, having been prais'd for bluntness, doth affect
A saucy roughness, and constrains the garb
Quite from his nature: he cannot flatter, he,
95 An honest mind and plain, he must speak truth:
An they will take it, so; if not, he's plain.
These kind of knaves I know, which in this plainness
Harbour more craft and more corrupter ends
Than twenty silly-ducking observants,
100 That stretch their duties nicely.
Kent. Sir, in good sooth, in sincere verity,

ACT II SCENE II

70　holy cords：sacred family ties.　**a-twain**：in two.

71　intrinse：intricate, tight.　**unloose**：undo.　**smooth**：flatter, fall in with.　**every**：用作复数代名词,故下行 rebel 为复数。

74　Renege：Deny.　**halcyon**：kingfisher,翠鸟。从前人们认为这种鸟的嘴总是朝着风的方向。

75　gale and vary：varying gale,重言法(hendiadys).此处指喜怒无常的心情。

76　nought：nothing.

77　epileptic：distorted and pale, as in an epileptic fit.

78　Smile you：Do you smile at?　**as**：as if.

79　Sarum：Salisbury. 附近有猎雁(wild goose)的沼泽地。

80　Camelot：传说中亚瑟王的宫廷所在地,据说在 Winchester 附近。Winchester goose 还有"妓女"之义。

83　antipathy：opposition in feeling or character.

86　likes：pleases.

88　occupation：business, habit.

92　affect：assume the manner of.

93—94　constrains the garb … nature：by an effort assumes a manner quite different from his real nature.

96　An：if.　**so**：well and good.

97　These：因接近 knaves 而用了复数。　**which**：who.

98　more corrupter：双重比较级,莎剧中常见。

99　silly-ducking observants：obsequious attendants foolishly bowing and scraping (observe = pay court to).

100　stretch … nicely：are over-particular in the performance of their duties.

Under the allowance of your grand aspect,
Whose influence, like the wreath of radiant fire
On flickering Phoebus' front, —

Cornwall.   What mean'st by this?

Kent. To go out of my dialect, which you discommend
so much. I know, sir, I am no flatterer: he that be-
guiled you in a plain accent was a plain knave; which
for my part I will not be, though I should win your
displeasure to entreat me to 't.

Cornwall. What was the offence you gave him?

Oswald. I never gave him any:
It pleas'd the king his master very late
To strike at me, upon his misconstruction;
When he, conjunct, and flattering his displeasure,
Tripp'd me behind; being down, insulted, rail'd,
And put upon him such a deal of man,
That worthied him, got praises of the king
For him attempting who was self-subdu'd;
And, in the fleshment of this dread exploit,
Drew on me here again.

Kent.   None of these rogues and cowards
But Ajax is their fool.

Cornwall.   Fetch forth the stocks!
You stubborn ancient knave, you reverend braggart,
We'll teach you.

Kent.   Sir, I am too old to learn,
Call not your stocks for me; I serve the king,
On whose employment I was sent to you;
You shall do small respect, show too bold malice
Against the grace and person of my master,
Stocking his messenger.

Cornwall. Fetch forth the stocks! As I have life and
honour, There shall he sit till noon.

Regan. Till noon! Till night, my lord; and all night too.

ACT II SCENE II

102 allowance: permission.　**aspect**: 重音在第二音节,此处含义双关语 1. appearance; 2. 星象术用语, the position of a star in relation to others as they appear to the observer on earth. Kent 故意用夸张而谄媚的语言把 Cornwall 比作天上的星宿。

103 influence: 中世纪认为从星星上流出的一种液体,影响人的命运。

104 flickering Phoebus' front: the forehead of Phoebus, the sun god, shining with unsteady light. 注意 flickering 用词不当,是故意用来与后面两个词凑成头韵(alliteration)以模仿浮华的文体的。　**mean'st**: do you mean.

105 my dialect: my usual way of speaking.　**discommend**: disapprove of.

106 he: 指 97 行提到的 these kind of knaves.

107 a plain knave: a real knave.

108—109 your displeasure: you, in your displeasure.

109 to 't: to do it, i.e. flatter you.

112 late: lately.

113 misconstruction: misunderstanding.

114 conjunct: joining in (with Lear).　**flattering**: encouraging.

115 being down, insulted: I being down, he insulted me.

116 put upon him: assumed.　**deal of man**: show of manliness.

117 worthied: ennobled.

118 him attempting who was self-subdu'd: attacking a man who attempted no resistance.

119 fleshment: excitement resulting from first success. 参见 II. ii 42。

120—121 None … their fool: All these rogues and cowards think even Ajax is a fool compared to them. Ajax 是荷马史诗《伊利亚特》中一位爱说大话的勇士。　**stocks**: 足枷。

122 reverend: grey-headed, old.

127 grace: honour.

128 Stocking: Putting in stocks.

129 As I have: As sure as I have.

Kent. Why, madam, if I were your father's dog,
You should not use me so.
Regan.   Sir, being his knave, I will.
Cornwall. This is a fellow of the self-same colour
135   Our sister speaks of. Come, bring away the stocks.
                                [*Stocks brought out.*
Gloucester. Let me beseech your Grace not to do so.
His fault is much, and the good king his master
Will check him for't: your purpos'd low correction
Is such as basest and contemned'st wretches
140   For pilferings and most common trespasses
Are punish'd with: the king must take it ill,
That he, so slightly valu'd in his messenger,
Should have him thus restrain'd.
Cornwall.   I'll answer that.
Regan. My sister may receive it much more worse
145   To have her gentleman abus'd, assaulted,
For following her affairs. Put in his legs.
                          [KENT *is put in the stocks.*
Come, my good lord, away.
                   [*Exeunt all but* GLOUCESTER *and* KENT.
Gloucester I am sorry for thee, friend; 'tis the duke's pleasure,
Whose disposition, all the world well knows,
150   Will not be rubb'd nor stopp'd: I'll entreat for thee.
Kent. Pray, do not, sir. I have watch'd and travell'd hard;
Some time I shall sleep out, the rest I'll whistle.
A good man's fortune may grow out at heels:
Give you good morrow!
155   *Gloucester.* The duke's to blame in this; 'twill be ill taken.   [*Exit.*
Kent. Good king, that must approve the common saw,
Thou out of heaven's benediction comest

ACT II SCENE II

133 should not use: would not treat. **being his knave**: just because you are his servant.

134 colour: kind.

135 bring away: bring along.

138 check: reprove. **purpos'd low correction**: intended shameful punishment.

139 contemned'st: most despised.

141 must: will (inevitably).

142 so slightly valu'd: so little respected.

143 restrain'd: confined. **answer**: answer for, take responsibility for.

144 more worse: 双重比较级。

146 following: carrying out.

148 pleasure: will.

150 rubb'd: hindered. 语出滚木游戏,地上坑坑洼洼的障碍叫rub.

151 watch'd: gone without sleep.

152 out: away.

153 out at heels: 一语双关:一方面说自己倒霉,一方面诙谐地指自己的脚踵被锁在足枷里。

154 Give: May God give.

155 ill taken: badly received.

156 approve: prove (the truth of). **saw**: proverb.

157—158 (英谚) Out of God's blessing into the warm sun, i.e. from better to worse. **warm**: hot, scorching.

To the warm sun.
Approach, thou beacon to this under globe,
160 That by thy comfortable beams I may
Peruse this letter. Nothing almost sees miracles But
misery: I know'tis from Cordelia,
Who hath most fortunately been inform'd
Of my obscured course; and shall find time
165 From this enormous state, seeking to give
Losses their remedies. All weary and o'er-watch'd,
Take vantage, heavy eyes, not to behold
This shameful lodging.
Fortune, good night, smile once more; turn thy wheel!
[*He sleeps*.

SCENE III

A PART OF THE HEATH

Enter EDGAR.

Edgar. I heard myself proclaim'd;
And by the happy hollow of a tree
Escap'd the hunt. No port is free; no place,
That guard, and most unusual vigilance,
5 Does not attend my taking. While I may 'scape
I will preserve myself; and am bethought
To take the basest and most poorest shape
That ever penury, in contempt of man,
Brought near to beast; my face I'll grime with filth,
10 Blanket my loins, elf all my hair in knots,
And with presented nakedness outface
The winds and persecutions of the sky.
The country gives me proof and precedent
Of Bedlam beggars, who with roaring voices,
15 Strike in their numb'd and mortified bare arms
Pins, wooden pricks, nails, sprigs of rosemary;
And with this horrible object, from low farms,

ACT II SCENE III

159 beacon: i.e. the sun. **this under globe**: the earth under heaven.

160 comfortable: comforting.

161—162 Miracles seldom happen except in times of misery. sees 等于 experiences.

164—166 obscured course: disguised attendance on Lear. **shall...remedies**: will find the opportunity to deliver us from this abnormal state of affairs, putting right what is wrong. **o'er-watch'd**: exhausted with sleeplessness.

167 vantage: advantage (of sleep).

168 This shameful lodging: i.e. The stocks he is imprisoned in.

169 wheel: 在中世纪人们的心目中,命运的形象是一只不停转动的巨轮,人在轮上,或升或降。

II. iii

1 proclaim'd: publicly announced as a wanted criminal (参见 II. i 61)。

2 happy: luckily found.

4 That: Where.

5 attend my taking: wait for my capture. **'scape**: escape.

6—7 am bethought/To take: intend to take.

7 most poorest: 双重最高级。

10 elf: tangle. 传说中淘气的小精灵常把马的鬃毛打成乱糟糟的结。

11 presented: exposed to view. **outface**: defy.

12 persecutions: harassments.

13 proof: experience.

14 Bedlam: cf. I. ii 136 行。

15 Strike: Drive. **mortified**: deadened, without feeling.

16 pricks: skewers. **rosemary**: 迷迭香(有刺)。

17 object: appearance, spectacle.

Poor pelting villages, sheep-cotes, and mills,
Sometime with lunatic bans, sometime with prayers.
20 Enforce their charity. Poor Turlygood! poor Tom!
That's something yet: Edgar I nothing am. [*Exit*.

SCENE IV

BEFORE GLOUCESTER'S CASTLE
KENT IN THE STOCKS

Enter LEAR, Fool, *and* Gentleman.

Lear. 'Tis strange that they should so depart from home,
And not send back my messenger.
Gentleman.   As I learn'd,
The night before there was no purpose in them
Of this remove.
Kent.   Hail to thee, noble master!
5 *Lear*. Ha!
Mak'st thou this shame thy pastime?
Kent.   No, my lord.
Fool. Ha, ha! he wears cruel garters. Horses are tied
by the head, dogs and bears by the neck, monkeys by
the loins, and men by the legs; when a man is over-
10 lusty at legs, then he wears wooden nether-stocks.
Lear. What's he that hath so much thy place mistook
To set thee here?
Kent.   It is both he and she,
Your son and daughter.
Lear. No.
15 *Kent*. Yes.
Lear. No, I say.
Kent. I say, yea.
Lear. No, No; they would not.
Kent. Yes, they have.

18 pelting: petty.

19 bans: banes, curses.

20 Enforce their charity: Compel others to show them charity.
Turlygood!: another name for a beggar.

21 Edgar…am: I am no longer Edgar.

II. iv

1 they: 指 Cornwall and Regan.

4 remove: removal, change of residence.

6 this shame: 指他被钉足枷的丑态。

7 cruel: ①painful; ②'crewel' = worsted yarn.

10 over-lusty at legs: 跑腿跑得太多。当时对流浪汉要逮捕惩罚。
nether-stocks: stockings, 与 upper stocks (=breeches) 相对而言,同时戏指足枷。

11—12 What's he … here?: Who is it that has misunderstood (mistaken) your. position (place) as my envoy so badly as to put you here?

13 son: son-in-law.

20 *Lear.* By Jupiter, I swear, no.
   Kent. By Juno, I swear, ay.
   Lear.   They durst not do 't;
      They could not, would not do 't; 'tis worse than murder,
      To do upon respect such violent outrage.
      Resolve me, with all modest haste, which way
25   Thou mightst deserve, or they impose, this usage,
      Coming from us.
   Kent.   My lord, when at their home
      I did commend your highness' letters to them,
      Ere I was risen from the place that show'd
      My duty kneeling, there came a reeking post,
30   Stew'd in his haste, half breathless, panting forth
      From Goneril his mistress salutations;
      Deliver'd letters, spite of intermission,
      Which presently they read: on whose contents
      They summon'd up their meiny, straight took horse;
35   Commanded me to follow, and attend
      The leisure of their answer; gave me cold looks:
      And meeting here the other messenger,
      Whose welcome, I perceiv'd, had poison'd mine, —
      Being the very fellow which of late
40   Display'd so saucily against your highness, —
      Having more man than wit about me, drew:
      He rais'd the house with loud and coward cries.
      Your son and daughter found this trespass worth
      The shame which here it suffers.
45 *Fool.* Winter's not gone yet, if the wild geese fly that way.
       Fathers that wear rags
         Do make their children blind,
       But fathers that bear bags
50   Shall see their children kind.

ACT II SCENE IV

21 durst not: would not dare.

23 upon respect: deliberately.

24 Resolve: Explain to. **modest**: becoming, appropriate. **which way**: in what way.

26 Coming from us: i.e. Since you are my messenger.

27 commend: hand over.

28 was risen: had risen.

29 reeking post: sweating messenger.

30 Stew'd: Cooked in hot sweat.

31 mistress: 所有格。

32 spite of intermission: in spite of the fact that he was interrupting me.

33 presently: immediately. **on whose contents**: on learning the contents of those letters.

34 meiny: many; followers, attendants. **straight**: straight away.

37 And meeting: And I, meeting.

38 Whose welcome: The reception of whom. **poison'd**: marred.

39 which: who.

40 Display'd: Showed off.

41 man: courage (cf. II. ii 116 行)。 **wit**: judgment. **drew**: I drew my sword. I 省略。

42 coward: cowardly.

43 worth: deserving.

45 i.e. We are not yet out of trouble.

48 blind: i.e. blind to filial duty.

49 bags: money-bags.

>   Fortune, that arrant whore,
>   Ne'er turns the key to the poor.
>
>   But for all this thou shalt have as many dolours for
>   thy daughters as thou canst tell in a year.
>
> *Lear.* O! how this mother swells up toward my heart;
> Hysterica passio! down, thou climbing sorrow!
> Thy element's below. Where is this daughter?
>
> *Kent.* With the earl, sir; here within.
>
> *Lear.* Follow me not; stay here.   [*Exit.*
>
> *Gentleman.* Made you no more offence than what you speak of?
>
> *Kent.* None.
>
>   How chance the king comes with so small a number?
>
> *Fool.* An thou hadst been set i' the stocks for that question, thou hadst well deserved it.
>
> *Kent.* Why, fool?
>
> *Fool.* We'll set thee to school to an ant, to teach thee there's no labouring i' the winter. All that follow their noses are led by their eyes but blind men; and there's not a nose among twenty but can smell him that's stinking. Let go thy hold when a great wheel runs down a hill, lest it break thy neck with following it; but the great one that goes up the hill, let him draw thee after. When a wise man give thee better counsel, give me mine again: I would have none but knaves follow it, since a fool gives it.
>
>   That sir which serves and seeks for gain,
>   And follows but for form,
>   Will pack when it begins to rain,
>   And leave thee in the storm.
>   But I will tarry; the fool will stay,
>   And let the wise man fly;
>   The knave turns fool that runs away;
>   The fool no knave, perdy.

51 arrant：notorious.

52 turns the key：opens the door.

53 for all this：nevertheless.　**dolours**：①girefs；②西班牙金币，dollars.　**for**：from, on account of.

54 tell：count.

55 mother：hysteria 的俗称。从前人们认为歇斯底里发病自胃部开始，逐渐上升，蔓延到全身。

56 Hysterica passio!：hysteria 的拉丁名称，passion 意为 suffering.

57 Thy element's below：Your proper place is low down in the abdomen（见 55 行）。

63 How chance：How does it happen that.　**number**：i.e. of attendants.

64 An：If.

67 set thee…ant：send you to the ant's school.

75 again：back.

77 That sir which：The man (gentleman) who.

78 for form：for the sake of appearance, i.e. not from true feelings of loyalty.

79 pack：pack up and go.

82 wise：i.e. worldly wise.

83—84 The knave…perdy：The knave who runs away turns into a real foo; but I, the Fool, shall not turn into a knave. 这里第一个 fool 是泛指，第二个 fool 则是特指，指 Fool 自己。knave 可解作仆人和坏蛋，双关。　**perdy**：出自法语 par Dieu＝by God.

85 *Kent.* Where learn'd you this, fool?
Fool. Not i' the stocks, fool.

Re-enter LEAR, *with* GLOUCESTER.

Lear. Deny to speak with me! They are sick! they are weary!
They have travell'd hard to-night! Mere fetches,
The images of revolt and flying off.
90 Fetch me a better answer.
Gloucester.   My dear lord,
You know the fiery quality of the duke;
How unremovable and fix'd he is
In his own course.
Lear. Vengeance! plague! death! confusion!
95 Fiery! what quality? Why, Gloucester, Gloucester,
I'd speak with the Duke of Cornwall and his wife.
Gloucester. Well, my good lord, I have inform'd them so.
Lear. Inform'd them! Dost thou understand me, man?
Gloucester. Ay, my good lord.
100 *Lear.* The king would speak with Cornwall; the dear father
Would with his daughter speak, commands her service:
Are they inform'd of this? My breath and blood!
Fiery! the fiery duke! Tell the hot duke that —
No, but not yet; may be he is not well:
105 Infirmity doth still neglect all office
Whereto our health is bound; we are not ourselves
When nature, being oppress'd, commands the mind
To suffer with the body. I'll forbear;
And am fall'n out with my more headier will,
110 To take the indispos'd and sickly fit
For the sound man. Death on my state! [*Looking on*

87 **Deny:** Refuse.
88 **fetches:** tricks, excuses.
89 **images:** tokens, indications. **flying off:** desertion.
91 **quality:** nature.
103 **hot:** hot-tempered.
105 **Infirmity:** A sick person. **still:** always. **office:** duty.
106 **Whereto... bound:** Which, if in health, we should feel bound to perform.
109 i.e. part with my first, impetuous idea.
110 **sickly fit:** man under an attack of sickness.
111 **state:** royal power.

KENT.] Wherefore
Should he sit here? This act persuades me
That this remotion of the duke and her
Is practice only. Give me my servant forth.
115 Go, tell the duke and 's wife I'd speak with them,
Now, presently: bid them come forth and hear me,
Or at their chamber-door I'll beat the drum
Till it cry sleep to death.
Gloucester. I would have all wel betwixt you.   [*Exit.*
120 *Lear.* O, me! my heart, my rising heart? but, down!
Fool. Cry to it, nuncle, as the cockney did to the eels
when she put 'em i' the paste alive; she knapped 'em o'
the coxcombs with a stick, and cried, 'Down, wantons, down!' 'Twas her brother that, in pure kind-
125 ness to his horse, buttered his hay.

Enter CORNWALL, REGAN, GLOUCESTER,
and Servants.

Lear. Good morrow to you both.
Cornwall.   Hail to your Grace.
                    [KENT *is set at liberty.*
Regan. I am glad to see your highness.
Lear. Regan, I think you are; I know what reason
I have to think so: if thou shouldst not be glad,
130 I would divorce me from thy mother's tomb,
Sepulchring an adultress. — [*To* KENT.] O! are you free?
Some other time for that. Beloved Regan,
Thy sister's naught: O Regan! she hath tied
Sharp-tooth'd unkindness, like a vulture, here:
                    [*Points to his heart.*
135 I can scare speak to thee; thou'lt not believe
With how deprav'd a quality — O Regan!

ACT II SCENE IV

112 **he**: 指 Kent.

113 **remotion**: removal (from their home).

114 **practice**: a trick. **forth**: i.e. out of the stocks.

116 **presently**: at once.

117 **chamber**: private apartment.

118 **cry sleep to death**: kills sleep with its noise.

121 **nuncle**: mine uncle. **cockney**: a silly woman (of London).

122 **paste**: pastry. **knapped**: rapped, struck.

123 **coxcombs**: heads. **wantons**: rogues.

125 **buttered his hay**: i.e. did something equally silly.

126 **Good morrow**: Good morning. 但说话时已是晚上,李尔是在讽刺他们姗姗来迟。

131 **Sepulchring**: (As it would then be) entombing. 全句的意思是说,要是 Regan 见了他不高兴,他只能认为她不是他的亲生女儿,而是她母亲与别人私通而生的私生女。

132 **that**: 指 Kent 被上足枷一事。李尔是说,这事另找时间再说。

133 **naught**: wicked.

134 **like a vulture**: 引用希腊神话典故,Prometheus 因盗火给人而受天帝之罚,绑在岩石上被鹫啄内脏,随啄随生。

135 **scarce**: scarcely.

136 **deprav'd**: corrupt, wicked. **quality**: manner (she treated me).

Regan. I pray you, sir, take patience. I have hope
You less know how to value her desert
Than she to scant her duty.
Lear. Say, how is that?
140 *Regan.* I cannot think my sister in the least
Would fail her obligation: if, sir, perchance
She have restrain'd the riots of your followers,
'Tis on such ground, and to such wholesome end,
As clears her from all blame.
145 *Lear.* My curses on her.
Regan. O, sir! you are old;
Nature in you stands on the very verge
Of her confine: you should be rul'd and led
By some discretion that discerns your state
Better than you yourself. Therefore I pray you
150 That to our sister you do make return;
Say, you have wrong'd her, sir.
Lear. Ask her forgiveness?
Do you but mark how this becomes the house:
'Dear daughter, I confess that I am old;
Age is unnecessary: on my knees I beg [*Kneeling.*
155 That you'll vouchsafe me raiment, bed, and food.'
Regan. Good sir, no more; these are unsightly tricks:
Return you to my sister.
Lear. [*Rising.*] Never, Regan.
She hath abated me of half my train;
Look'd black upon me; struck me with her tongue,
160 Most serpent-like, upon the very heart.
All the stor'd vengeances of heaven fall
On her ingrateful top! Strike her young bones,
You taking airs, with lameness!
Cornwall. Fie, sir, fie!
Lear. You nimble lightnings, dart your blinding flames
165 Into her scornful eyes! Infect her beauty,

ACT II SCENE IV

138　**desert**: merits.

139　**to scant**: to neglect. 前面省略了 knows how.

143　**ground**: sufficient reason.　**wholesome**: beneficial.

146—147　**Nature ... confine**: i.e. Your life is nearly at an end. **confine**: boundary, utmost limit.

148　**discretion**: discreet person.　**state**: condition.

150　**make return**: return.

152　**becomes the house**: befits the household.

154　**Age is unnecessary**: Old people are useless.

158　**abated**: curtailed, deprived.

161　句首省略 May.

162　**top**: head.　**young bones**: unborn children.

163　**taking**: infectious, carrying diseases that 'take' people. 此句结构为 May airs strike…

KING LEAR

>   You fen-suck'd fogs, drawn by the powerful sun,
>   To fall and blast her pride!
>   *Regan.* O the blest gods! So will you wish on me,
>   When the rash mood is on.
> 170 *Lear.* No, Regan, thou shalt never have my curse:
>   Thy tender-hefted nature shall not give
>   Thee o'er to harshness: her eyes are fierce, but thine
>   Do comfort and not burn. 'Tis not in thee
>   To grudge my pleasures, to cut off my train,
> 175 To bandy hasty words, to scant my sizes,
>   And, in conclusion, to oppose the bolt
>   Against my coming in: thou better know'st
>   The offices of nature, bond of childhood,
>   Effects of courtesy, dues of gratitude;
> 180 Thy half o' the kingdom hast thou not forgot,
>   Wherein I thee endow'd
>   *Regan.*   Good sir, to the purpose.
>   *Lear.* Who put my man i' the stocks?   [*Tucket within.*
>   *Cornwall.*   What trumpet's that?
>   *Regan.* I know't, my sister's; this approves her letter,
>   That she would soon be here. Is your lady come?

Enter OSWALD.

> 185 *Lear.* This is a slave, whose easy-borrow'd pride
>   Dwells in the fickle grace of her he follows.
>   Out, varlet, from my sight!
>   *Cornwall.*   What means your Grace?

Enter GONERIL.

>   *Lear.* Who stock'd my servant? Regan, I have good hope
>   Thou didst not know on't. Who comes here? O heavens,
> 190 If you do love old men, if your sweet sway

- 166 **fen-suck'd**: sucked up from swamps.
- 171 **tender-hefted**: set in tender bodily frame (haft), gentle.
- 175 **scant**: reduce. **sizes**: allowances.
- 176 **oppose the bolt**: set the bolt, bar the door.
- 178 **offices**: duties.
- 179 **Effects**: manifestations, forms.
- 180 **forgot**: forgotten.
- 181 **Wherein**: with which. **to the purpose**: come to the point.
- 183 **approves**: confirms.
- 184 **Is...come**: Has...come. 运动动词多用 be 加 p.p. 的形式。
- 185 **easy-borrow'd**: assumed without deserts.
- 186 **fickle grace**: unreliable favour.
- 189 **on't**: of it.

Allow obedience, if yourselves are old,
Make it your cause; send down and take my part!
[*To* GONERIL.] Art not asham'd to look upon this beard?
O Regan, wilt thou take her by the hand?
Goneril. Why not by the hand, sir? How have I offended?
All's not offence that indiscretion finds
And dotage terms so.
Lear.   O sides! you are too tough;
Will you yet hold? How came my man i' the stocks?
Cornwall. I set him there, sir; but his own disorders
Deserv'd much less advancement.
Lear.   You! did you?
Regan. I pray you, father, being weak, seem so.
If, till the expiration of your month,
You will return and sojourn with my sister,
Dismissing half your train, come then to me;
I am now from home, and out of that provision
Which shall be needful for your entertainment.
Lear. Return to her? and fifty men dismiss'd!
No, rather I abjure all roofs, and choose
To wage against the enmity o' the air;
To be a comrade with the wolf and owl,
Necessity's sharp pinch! Return with her!
Why, the hot-blooded France, that dowerless took
Our youngest born. I could as well be brought
To knee his throne, and, squire-like, pension beg
To keep base life afoot. Return with her!
Persuade me rather to be slave and sumpter
To this detested groom.   [*Pointing at* OSWALD.
Goneril.   At your choice, sir.
Lear. I prithee, daughter, do not make me mad;
I will not trouble thee, my child; farewell.

ACT II SCENE IV

191 Allow: Approve.

192 it: old age. **send down**: i.e., your messengers.

196 indiscretion: bad judgment. **finds**: holds.

197 terms: calls. **sides**: A side is the part of the body between armpit and hip. Lear 指的是自己的身体居然结实得能承受如此巨大的打击。

199 disorders: disorderly acts.

200 much less advancement: still worse treatment.

201 seem so: behave accordingly.

205 from: away from. **out of**: without.

209 wage against: contend with.

214 knee: kneel before. **squire-like**: like a dependant attendant.

214—215 pension…afoot: beg for an allowance to keep me alive. **afoot**: on foot, active in being.

216 sumpter: pack-horse, beast of burden.

<pre>
220   We'll no more meet, no more see one another;
       But yet thou art my flesh, my blood, my daughter;
       Or rather a disease that's in my flesh,
       Which I must needs call mine: thou art a boil,
       A plague-sore, an embossed carbuncle,
225   In my corrupted blood. But I'll not chide thee;
       Let shame come when it will. I do not call it:
       I do not bid the thunder-bearer shoot,
       Nor tell tales of thee to high-judging Jove.
       Mend when thou canst; be better at thy leisure:
230   I can be patient; I can stay with Regan,
       I and my hundred knights.
         Regan.   Not altogether so:
       I look'd not for you yet, nor am provided
       For your fit welcome. Give ear, sir, to my sister;
       For those that mingle reason with your passion
235   Must be content to think you old, an so —
       But she knows what she does.
         Lear.   Is this well spoken?
         Regan. I dare avouch it, sir: what! fifty followers?
       Is it not well? What should you need of more?
       Yea, or so many, sith that both charge and danger
240   Speak 'gainst so great a number? How, in one house,
       Should many people, under two commands,
       Hold amity? 'Tis hard; almost impossible.
         Goneril. Why might not you, my lord, receive attendance
       From those that she calls servants, or from mine?
245   Regan. Why not, my lord? If then they chanc'd to slack you
       We could control them. If you will come to me,
       For now I spy a danger, I entreat you
       To bring but five-and-twenty; to no more
       Will I give place or notice.
</pre>

ACT II SCENE IV

224 embossed: swollen.

227 the thunder-bearer: 罗马神话中的主神 Jove (Jupiter), 他以雷作武器。 **shoot**: strike with thunderbolt.

228 high-judging: supreme judge or judge in heaven.

229 Mend: reform, improve yourself.

234 mingle…passion: bring reason to bear on your passion.

239 sith that: since. **charge**: the expense. **danger**: i.e. of disturbance.

242 amity: friendship.

245 slack you: be inattentive in their service to you.

249 notice: recognition.

250   *Lear.* I gave you all —
     Regan.   And in good time you gave it.
     Lear. Made you my guardians, my depositaries,
        But kept a reservation to be follow'd
        With such a number. What! must I come to you
        With five-and-twenty? Regan, said you so?
255   *Regan.* And speak't again, my lord; no more with me.
     Lear. Those wicked creatures yet do look well-favour'd,
        When others are more wicked; not being the worst
        Stands in some rank of praise. [*To* GONERIL.] I'll go with thee:
        Thy fifty yet doth double five-and-twenty,
260   And thou art twice her love.
     Goneril.   Hear me, my lord.
     What need you five-and-twenty, ten, or five,
     To follow in a house, where twice so many
     Have a command to tend you?
     Regan.   What need one?
     Lear. O! reason not the need; our basest beggars
265   Are in the poorest thing superfluous:
     Allow not nature more than naturte needs,
     Man's life is cheap as beast's. Thou art a lady;
     If only to go warm were gorgeous,
     Why, nature needs not what thou gorgeous wear'st,
270   Which scarcely keeps thee warm. But, for true need, —
     You heavens, give me that patience, patience I need!
     You see me here, you gods, a poor old man,
     As full of grief as age; wretched in both!
     If it be you that stir these daughters' hearts
275   Against their father, fool me not so much
     To beat it tamely; touch me with noble anger,
     And let not women's weapons, water-drops,
     Stain my man's cheeks! No, you unnatural hags,

ACT II SCENE IV

251   depositaries: trustees.

252   kept a reservation: make a saving clause or condition (see I. i 132).

253   With: By.

256   well-favour'd: good-looking.

258   Stands…praise: is to some extent praiseworthy (i.e. Goneril is at least better than Regan).

260   art twice her love: show me twice as much love.

264   reason not: don't argue about.

265   superfluous: possessing more than they need.

266   Allow not nature: If you don't allow man to possess.

267   cheap as: of as little value as.

268—270   i.e. If the need for warmth were the only purpose of wearing clothes, well, your body does not need the fine clothes you wear — which hardly keep you warm.

270   for true need: as for what I really need most.

273   both: both grief and age.

275—276   fool me…To: do not make me such a fool as to.

276   touch: imbue.

277   water-drops: tears.

I will have such revenges on you both
That all the world shall — I will do such things, —
What they are yet I know not, — but they shall be
The terrors of the earth. You think I'll weep;
No, I'll not weep:
I have full cause of weeping, but this heart
Shall break into a hundred thousand flaws
Or ere I'll weep. O fool! I shall go mad.
           [*Exeunt* LEAR, GLOUCESTER, KENT, *and* Fool.
Cornwall. Let us withdraw; 'twill be a storm.
                    [*Storm heard at a distance*.
Regan. This house is little; the old man and his people
Cannot be well bestow'd.
Goneril. 'Tis his own blame; hath put himself from rest,
And must needs taste his folly.
Regan. For his particular, I'll receive him gladly,
But not one follower.
Goneril.   So am I purpos'd.
Where is my Lord of Gloucester?
Cornwall. Follow'd the old man forth. He is return'd.

Re-enter GLOUCESTER.

Gloucester. The king is in high rage.
Cornwall.   Whither is he going?
Gloucester. He calls to horse; but will I know not whither.
Cornwall. 'Tis best to give him way; he leads himself.
Goneril. My lord, entreat him by no means to stay.
Gloucester. Alack! the night comes on, and the bleak winds
Do sorely ruffle; for many miles about
There's scarce a bush.
Regan.   O! sir, to wilful men,

ACT II SCENE IV

284 **cause of weeping**: reason to weep.
285 **flaws**: pieces, fragments.
286 **Or ere**: before.
287 **'twill be**: there will be.
289 **bestow'd**: accommodated.
290 **hath**: he has. **from rest**: away from where he might rest.
292 **his particular**: himself alone.
295 **Follow'd**: He has followed. **is return'd**: has returned.
297 **calls to horse**: calls "To horse!" **will**: will go.
298 **give him way**: let him be. **leads himself**: is his own master.
299 **by no means**: 按正常词序应在 entreat 之前。
301 **ruffle**: bluster, rage.
302 **scarce**: scarcely.

The injuries that they themselves procure
Must be their schoolmasters. Shut up your doors;
305 He is attended with a desperate train
And what they may incense him to, being apt
To have his ear abus'd, wisdom bids fear.
Cornwall. Shut up your doors, my lord; 'tis a wild night:
My Regan counsels well: come out o' the storm.

[*Exeunt.*

ACT II SCENE IV

303 themselves procure: bring on themselves.
305 with: by.
306 incense: incite.
307 abus'd: deceived, misled by ill advice.

ACT III

SCENE I

A HEATH

A storm, with thunder and lightning. Enter
KENT *and a* Gentleman, *meeting*.

Kent. Who's here, beside foul weather?
Gentleman. One minded like the weather, most unquietly.
Kent. I know you. Where's the king?
Gentleman. Contending with the fretful elements;
5   Bids the wind blow the earth into the sea,
     Or swell the curled waters 'bove the main,
     That things might change or cease; tears his white hair,
     Which the impetuous blasts, with eyeless rage,
     Catch in their fury, and make nothing of;
10   Strives in his little world of man to out-scorn
     The to-and-fro-conflicting wind and rain.
     This night, wherein the cub-drawn bear would couch,
     The lion and the belly-pinched wolf
     Keep their fur dry, unbonneted the runs,
15   And bids what will take all.
Kent.   But who is with him?
Gentleman. None but the fool, who labours to out-jest
     His heart-struck injuries.
Kent.   Sir, I do know you;
     And dare, upon the warrant of my note,
     Commend a dear thing to you. There is division.
20   Although as yet the face of it be cover'd
     With mutual cunning, 'twixt Albany and Cornwall;

III. i

   2 **One minded**: Someone whose mind is troubled.

   4 **fretful elements**: tempestuous wind and rain.

   6 **curled waters**: curly waves. **'bove**: above. **main**: mainland.

   7 **That**: So that. **things**: the state of affairs in general.

   8 **eyeless**: blind.

   9 **make nothing of**: show to respect for.

  10 **his little…man**：在莎士比亚时代，人被看作是微观世界（microcosm），相对于自然的宏观世界（macrocosm）。

  12 **cub-drawn**: sucked dry by her cubs and hence hungry. **couch**: lie down.

  13 **belly-pinched**: pinched in the stomach, straving.

  14 **unbonneted**: bare-headed.

  15 **what**: whoever. **take all**：赌徒孤注一掷时的喊声，"谁要谁就都拿去"。

  16 **out-jest**: jest him out of.

  17 **heart-struck**: which have struck him to the heart.

  18 **upon…note**: on the strength of my knowing you.

  19 **Commend**: entrust. **dear**: important. **division**: disagreement.

Who have—as who have not, that their great stars
Thron'd and set high? — servants, who seem no less,
Which are to France the spies and speculations
25 Intelligent of our state; what hath been seen,
Either in snuffs and packings of the dukes,
Or the hard rein which both of them have borne
Against the old kind king; or something deeper,
Whereof perchance these are but furnishings;
30 But, true it is, from France there comes a power
Into this scatter'd kingdom; who already,
Wise in our negligence, have secret feet
In some of our best ports, and are at point
To show their open banner. Now to you:
35 If on my credit you dare build so far
To make your speed to Dover, you shall find
Some that will thank you, making just report
Of how unnatural and bemadding sorrow
The king hath cause to plain.
40 I am a gentleman of blood and breeding,
And from some knowledge and assurance offer
This office to you.

Gentleman. I will talk further with you.

Kent.   No, do not.
For confirmation that I am much more
45 Than my out-wall, open this purse, and take
What it contains. If you shall see Cordelia, —
As doubt not but you shall, — show her this ring,
And she will tell you who your fellow is
That yet you do not know. Fie on this storm!
50 I will go seek the king.

Gentleman. Give me your hand. Have you no more to say?

Kent. Few words, but, to effect, more than all yet;
That, when we have found the king, — in which your

ACT III SCENE I

22 that their: whose. **great stars**: fortunes. 后省略 are.
23 seem no less: at any rate appear to be servants.
24 Which are: But who are. **speculations**: observers, watchers.
25 Intelligent of: Giving information about.
26 snuffs: resentments, quarrels. **packings**: plots.
27 hard rein ... borne: cruel way in which both of them have acted. bear hard rein against 原意为勒紧马的缰绳。
29 furnishings: trimmings.
30 power: army.
31 scatter'd: divided. **who**: 指 power.
32 Wise in our negligence: Aware of our negligence. **feet**: footings.
33 at point: on the point, ready.
34 Now to you: Now to come to your part.
35 on my credit ... build: you dare trust me. **build on**: 意为 depend on.
36 To: As to. **Dover**: 为英国东岸与法国隔海相望最近的港口。
37 making: when you make. **just**: accurate.
38 bemadding: maddening.
39 plain: complain of.
41 assurance: confidence.
45 out-wall: outward appearance.
47 but: that.
48 your fellow: i.e., myself.
52 to effect: with a view to effect, in their consequences.

118 **KING LEAR**

        pain
        That way, I'll this, — he that first lights on him
55   Holla the other.

                              [*Exeunt severally.*

SCENE II

ANOTHER PART OF THE HEATH STORM STILL

Enter LEAR *and* Fool.

  Lear. Blow, winds, and crack your cheeks! rage! blow!
  You cataracts and hurricanoes, spout
  Till you have drench'd our steeples, drown'd the cocks!
  You sulphurous and thought-executing fires,
5 Vaunt-couriers to oak-cleaving thunderbolts,
  Singe my white head! And thou, all-shaking thunder,
  Strike flat the thick rotundity o' the world!
  Crack nature's moulds, all germens spill at once
  That make ingrateful man!
10 *Fool.* O nuncle, court holy-water in a dry house is better than this rain-water out o' door. Good nuncle, in, and ask thy daughters' blessing; here's a night pities neither wise man nor fool.
  Lear. Rumble thy bellyful! Spit, fire! spout, rain!
15 Nor rain, wind, thunder, fire, are my daughters:
  I tax not you, you elements, with unkindness;
  I never gave you kingdom, call'd you children,
  You owe me no subscription: then, let fall
  Your horrible pleasure; here I stand, your slave,
20 A poor, infirm, weak, and despis'd old man.
  But yet I call you servile ministers,
  That have with two pernicious daughters join'd

ACT III SCENE II

53 pain: effort, i.e., search.
54 lights on: comes upon by chance.
55 Holla: shout.

III. ii

2 cataracts: waterspouts (from heaven). **hurricanoes**: 'hurricanes'的另一形式。

3 cocks: 屋顶上的 weathercocks.

4 thought-executing fires: lightning as swift as thought.

5 Vaunt-couriers: Advance scourts, 转义 messengers, heralds.

8 nature's moulds: the moulds used by nature in forming men. **germens**: seeds. **spill**: destroy.

9 ingrateful: ungrateful.

10 nuncle: mine uncle 连读时的简称形式, 弄人对君主的称呼。 **court holy-water**: flattery (a common phrase at the time).

12 ask…blessing: apologize to and make peace with your daughters. **pities**: 前省略 that.

16 tax: accuse, charge (cf. I. iv 338 and notes), 下接 with 短语。

18 subscription: submission, obedience.

19 pleasure: will, desire.

21 ministers: agents.

Your high-engender'd battles 'gainst a head
So old and white as this. O! O! 'tis foul.

25 *Fool.* He that has a house to put his head in has a good head-piece.

    The cod-piece that will house
        Before the head has any,
    The head and he shall louse;
30   So beggars marry many.
    The man that makes his toe
        What he his heart should make,
    Shall of a corn cry woe,
        And turn his sleep to wake.

35 For there was never yet fair woman but she made mouths in a glass.

Enter KENT.

Lear. No, I will be the pattern of all patience;
I will say nothing.
Kent. Who's there?
40 *Fool.* Marry, here's grace and a cod-piece; that's a wise man and a fool.
Kent. Alas! sir, are you here? Things that love night
Love not such nights as these; the wrathful skies
Gallow the very wanderers of the dark,
45 And make them keep their caves. Since I was man
Such sheets of fire, such bursts of horrid thunder,
Such groans of roaring wind and rain, I never
Remember to have heard; man's nature cannot carry
The affliction nor the fear.
Lear.   Let the great gods,
50 That keep this dreadful pother o'er our heads,
Find out their enemies now. Tremble, thou wretch,
That hast within thee undivulged crimes,
Unwhipp'd of justice; hide thee, thou bloody hand;

23　high-engender'd battles：battalions bred in the sky.

26　head-piece：both head-covering and brain.

27　cod-piece：十五、十六世纪时男子紧身裤前开口处上面的口盖，此处指男子生殖器。　**house**：动词，此处作 seek entry，即 seek to have intercourse 解。

28　any：any house.

29　louse：be lousy, infected with lice.

30　So…many：Many beggars marry in this way.

27—30　i.e. The man who satisfies his sexual appetites before he has a house to live in will end up by marrying a wife and becoming infected with lice.

31　makes：is occupied with.

31—34　i.e. The man who pays more attention to his toe (an unimportant part of his body) than to his heart (a vital part) will suffer grievously from a corn（鸡眼）and will be kept awake when he wants to sleep.

34　wake（n.）：sleeplessness.

35—36　made mouths：made faces, preened herself.

36　glass：mirror.

37　pattern：model.

40　grace：the king's grace.　**cod-piece**：见 27 行注，在丑服饰中此物最明显。

44　Gallow（v.t.）：Frighten, Terrify，方言。　**wanderers…dark**：wild beasts which roam in the dark.

45　keep…caves：cf. III.i 12—14.

48　carry：bear, endure.

50　pother：tumult, commotion.

51　Find…now：i.e. discover the godless by their fear.

52　undivulged：unrevealed, hidden.

53　of：by.

Thou perjur'd, and thou simular of virtue
55 That art incestuous; caitiff, to pieces shake,
That under covert and convenient seeming
Hast practis'd on man's life; close pent-up guilts,
Rive your concealing continents, and cry
These dreadful summoners grace. I am a man
60 More sinn'd against than sinning.
Kent.   Alack! bare-headed!
Gracious my lord, hard by here is a hovel;
Some friendship will it lend you 'gainst the tempest;
Repose you there while I to this hard house, —
More harder than the stone whereof 'tis rais'd, —
65 Which even but now, demanding after you,
Denied me to come in, return and force
Their scanted courtesy.
Lear.   My wits begin to turn.
Come on, my boy. How dost, my boy? Art cold?
I am cold myself. Where is this straw, my fellow?
70 The art of our necessities is strange,
That can make vile things precious. Come, your hovel.
Poor fool and knave, I have one part in my heart
That's sorry yet for thee.
Fool.

        He that has a little tiny wit,
75   With hey, ho, the wind and the rain,
        Must make content with his fortunes fit,
           Though the rain it raineth every day.

Lear. True, my good boy. Come, bring us to this hovel.   [*Exeunt* LEAR *and* KENT.
Fool. This is a brave night to cool a courtezan.
80 I'll speak a prophecy ere I go:
        When priests are more in word than matter;
        When brewers mar their malt with water;

54 perjur'd: perjurer, 做伪证者。　**simular of**: simulator of, pretender to.

55 caitiff: wretch.　**to pieces shake**: i.e. shake with fear and trembling.

56 covert: secret.　**seeming**: pretence, hypocrisy.

57 practis'd on: plotted against.　**close**(adv.): secretly.　**guilts**: crimes.

58 Rive...continents: burst open the covering that hides you.

58—59 cry...grace: beg mercy from.　**summoners**: officers who summon to justice.

60 Alack: Alas.

61 hard by: very near.

62 lend: provide.

63 hard house: cruel household.

64 More harder: 双重比较级，more 为强调词。　**rais'd**: built.

65 demanding after: asking for.

66 Denied...in: refused me admittance.　**force**: urge, press for.

67 scanted: stingy.　**wits**: mental faculties, mind.　**turn**: whirl, become giddy.

68 How dost (thou): How are you?

69 straw: hovel, an open shelter thatched with straw.

70 art: power of transforming, like alchemy.

71 vile: worthless.

76 make...fit: make content (desire, satisfaction) fit his fortunes, i.e. be content with his fortunes.

79 brave: fine, 反话。

81 more...matter: preach more than they practise.

82 mar: adulterate.　**malt**: malt liquor, 大麦浸泡发芽，其水发酵，为制啤酒的半成品。

124   KING LEAR

       When nobles are their tailors' tutors;
       No heretics burn'd, but wenches' suitors;
85   When every case in law is right;
       No squire in debt, nor no poor knight;
       When slanders do not live in tongues;
       Nor cutpurses come not to throngs;
       When usurers tell their gold i' the field;
90   And bawds and whores do churches build;
       Then shall the realm of Albion
       Come to great confusion;
       Then comes the time, who lives to see 't.
       That going shall be us'd with feet.
95 This prophecy Merlin shall make; for I live before his time.   [*Exit*.

SCENE III

A ROOM IN GLOUCESTER'S CASTLE

Enter GLOUCESTER *and* EDMUND.

Gloucester. Alack, alack! Edmund, I like not this unnatural dealing. When I desired their leave that I might pity him, they took from me the use of mine own house; charged me, on pain of their perpetual
5 displeasure, neither to speak of him, entreat for him, nor any way sustain him.

Edmund. Most savage, and unnatural!

Gloucester. Go to; say you nothing. There is division between the dukes, and a worse matter than that. I
10 have received a letter this night; 'tis dangerous to be spoken; I have locked the letter in my closet. These injuries the king now bears will be revenged home; there's part of a power already footed; we must incline to the king. I will seek him and privily relieve him;
15 go you and maintain talk with the duke, that my charity be not of him perceived. If he ask for me, I

ACT III SCENE III

83 are…tutors: teach their tailors how to make clothes.
84 burn'd: 双关 1.(异教徒)被烧死；2.(嫖客)生杨梅疮。
86 no poor knight: no knight poor.
87 live: become lively.
88 Nor…throngs: and pickpockets do not move about among crowds.
89 tell: count. **i' the field**: i.e. in the open.
90 build: as a sign of repentance.
91 Albion: England, 源自古凯尔特语。
93 who lives: for whoever lives.
94 going…feet: feet shall be used for walking.
95 Merlin: 亚瑟王及其圆桌骑士的传说中的巫师,善作预言。此处故意让弄臣自称为古人来开玩笑。

III. iii

2 unnatural dealing: unkind treatment. **leave**: permission.
3 pity: show pity to, i.e. relieve. **him**: 指 Lear.
4 pain: penalty.
6 any way: in any way. **sustain**: care for.
8 Go to: come! **division**: contention, conflict.
9 a worse matter: i.e. the French invasion, which is much graver than the dispute between Cornwall and Albany.
11 spoken: spoken of. **closet**: private cabinet for papers.
12 home(adv.): fully.
13 power: force. **footed**: gained a footing.
13—14 incline to: side with.
14 privily relieve: secretly help.
15 that: so that.
16 of him: by him.

am ill and gone to bed. If I die for it, as no less is
threatened me, the king, my old master, must be
relieved. There is some strange thing toward,
20   Edmund; pray you, be careful.   [*Exit.*
Edmund. This courtesy, forbid thee, shall the duke
Instantly know; and of that letter too:
This seems a fair deserving, and must draw me
That which my father loses; no less than all:
25   The younger rises when the old doth fall.   [*Exit.*

SCENE IV

THE HEATH BEFORE A HOVEL

Enter LEAR, KENT, *and* Fool.

Kent. Here is the place, my lord; good my lord, enter:
The tyranny of the open night's too rough
For nature to endure.   [*Storm still.*
Lear.   Let me alone.
Kent. Good my lord, enter here.
Lear.   Wilt break my heart?
5   *Kent.* I'd rather break mine own. Good my lord, enter.
Lear. Thou think'st 'tis much that this contentious storm
Inavdes us to the skin: so 'tis to thee;
But where the greater malady is fix'd,
The lesser is scarce felt. Thou'dst shun a bear;
10   But if thy flight lay toward the roaring sea,
Thou'dst meet the bear i' the mouth. When the mind's free
The body's delicate; the tempest in my mind
Doth from my senses take all feeling else
Save what beats there. Filial ingratitude!
15   Is it not as this mouth should tear this hand
For lifting food to 't? But I will punish home:

ACT III SCENE IV

 17 **as**: for indeed.

 18 **threatened**: threatened against.

 19 **is…things**: 单数动词在前，复数主语在后，这是常用法。 **toward**: imminent, about to happen.

 21 **courtesy, forbid thee**: kindness which was forbidden you.

 23 **deserving**: service which will deserve to be rewarded. **draw me**: bring into my hands.

III. iv

 2 **the open night**: night in the open.

 3 **nature**: human nature, man.

 4 **Wilt…heart**: i.e. As physical distress has distracted Lear from his heartbreak, insisting that he enter the hovel will make his heart break.

 6 **contentious**: quarrelsome, contending with us.

 8 **fix'd**: driven in, lodged.

 9 **scarce**: scarcely.

 11 **Thou'dst**: You would. **i' the mouth**: face to face. **free**: at ease.

 12 **delicate**: sensitive to discomfort.

 13—14 **all…Save**: all other feelings except.

 14 **beats**: ①throbs, thinks laboriously; ②rages, as of a tempest. **there**: i.e. in my mind.

 15 **as**: as if.

 16 **home**(adv.): fully.

No, I will weep no more. In such a night
To shut me out! Pour on; I will endure.
In such a night as this! O Regan, Goneril!
20   Your old kind father, whose frank heart gave all,
O! that way madness lies; let me shun that;
No more of that.
Kent. Good, my lord, enter here.
Lear. Prithee, go in thyself; seek thine own ease;
This tempest will not give me leave to ponder
25   On things would hurt me more. But I'll go in.
[*To the* Fool.] In, boy; go first. You houseless poverty, —
Nay, get thee in. I'll pray, and then I'll sleep.
[Fool *goes in.*
Poor naked wretches, wheresoe'er you are,
That bide the pelting of this pitiless storm,
30   How shall your houseless heads and unfed sides,
Your loop'd and window'd raggedness, defend you
From seasons such as these? O! I have ta'en
Too little care of this. Take physic, pomp;
Expose thyself to feel what wretches feel,
35   That thou mayst shake the superflux to them,
And show the heavens more just.
Edgar. [*Within.*] Fathom and half, fathom and half!
Poor Tom! [*The* Fool *runs out from the hovel.*
Fool. Come not in here, nuncle; here's a spirit.
Help me! help me!
40   *Kent.* Give me thy hand. Who's there?
Fool. A spirit, a spirit: he says his name's poor Tom.
Kent. What art thou that dost grumble there i' the straw?
Come forth.

20 frank: liberal, generous.

23 ease: comfort, protection.

24 leave: permission.

25 would: 前省略 that.

26 poverty: poor people, 抽象名词用作具体名词。

29 bide: endure.

30 sides: stomachs.

31 loop'd...raggedness: clothes full of holes.

32 seasons: spells of bad weathers. **ta'en**: taken.

33 Take physic, pomp: Take this medicine, you who live in a world of luxury. **pomp**: 在这里是拟人化的祈使对象。

35 shake: send or scatter by shaking. **the superflux**: your superfluity.

36 show: 后省略 that. **heavens**: 后省略 are.

37 Fathom and half: 原为水手在测水深时的呼喊。 **Poor Tom**: cf. II. iii 20.

Enter EDGAR *disguised as a madman.*

Edgar. Away! the foul fiend follows me!
Through the sharp hawthorn blow the winds.
Hum! go to thy cold bed and warm thee.
Lear. Didst thou give all to thy two daughters?
And art thou come to this?
Edgar. Who gives anything to poor Tom? whom the foul fiend bath led through fire and through flame, through ford and whirlpool, o'er bog and quagmire; that hath laid knives under his pillow, and halters in his pew; set ratsbane by his porridge; made him proud of heart, to ride on a bay trotting-horse over four-inched bridges, to course his own shadow for a traitor. Bless thy five wits! Tom's a-cold. O! do de, do de, do de. Bless thee from whirlwinds, star-blasting, and taking! Do poor Tom some charity, whom the foul fiend vexes. There could I have him now, and there, and there again, and there. [*Storm still.*
Lear. What! have his daughters brought him to this pass?
Couldst thou save nothing? Didst thou give them all?
Fool. Nay, he reserved a blanket, else we had been all shamed.
Lear. Now all the plagues that in the pendulous air
Hang fated o'er men's faults light on thy daughters!
Kent. He hath no daughters, sir.
Lear. Death, traitor! nothing could have subdu'd nature.
To such a lowness, but his unkind daughters.
Is it the fashion that discarded fathers
Should have thus little mercy on their flesh?
Judicious punishment! 'twas this flesh begot
Those pelican daughters.

ACT III SCENE IV

52 halters：绞索。

52—56 魔鬼引诱人自杀的几种方法。

53 pew：gallery, seat. **porridge**：broth.

54 bay：栗色的。

55 four-inched：four inches wide. **course**：pursue.

56 five wits：the five faculties of common sense, imagination, fantasy, estimation and memory.

56—57 do…de：发抖时发出的声音。

57—58 star-blasting：being struck by the evil influence of stars. **taking**：infection (cf. II. iv 163).

59 There：Edgar 假装魔鬼在他身上到处乱咬。

61 pass：miserable plight.

65 all：前省略 may. **pendulous**：over-hanging.

66 fated：having the power of fate. **light**：alight, fall.

68 subdu'd nature：reduced his natural powers.

69 unkind：unnatural (also suggesting 'cruel').

72 begot：前省略 that.

73 pelican：young pelicans were supposed to feed on their mothers' life-blood, or strike at the breasts of the old birds to drain their life out.

Edgar. Pillicock sat on Pillicock-hill:
      Halloo, halloo, loo, loo!

Fool. This cold night will turn us all to fools and madmen.

Edgar. Take heed o' the foul fiend. Obey thy parents; keep thy word justly; swear not; commit not with man's sworn spouse; set not thy sweet heart on proud array. Tom's a-cold.

Lear. What hast thou been?

Edgar. A servingman, proud in heart and mind; that curled my hair, wore gloves in my cap, served the lust of my mistress's heart, and did the act of darkness with her; swore as many oaths as I spake words, and broke them in the sweet face of heaven; one that slept in the contriving of lust, and waked to do it. Wine loved I deeply, dice dearly, and in woman out-paramoured the Turk: false of heart, light of ear, bloody of hand; hog in sloth, fox in stealth, wolf in greediness, dog in madness, lion in prey. Let not the creaking of shoes nor the rustling of silks betray thy poor heart to woman: keep thy foot out of brothels, thy hand out of plackets, thy pen from lenders' books, and defy the foul fiend. Still through the hawthorn blows the cold wind; says suum, mum ha no nonny. Dolphin my boy, my boy; sessa! let him trot by.

[*Storm still.*

Lear. Why, thou wert better in thy grave than to answer with thy uncovered body this extremity of the skies. Is man no more than this? Consider him well. Thou owest the worm no silk, the beast no hide, the sheep no wool, the cat no perfume. Ha! here's three on 's are sophisticated; thou art the thing itself; unaccommodated man is no more but such a poor, bare, forked animal as thou art. Off, off, you lendings!

74　Pillcock：penis. 此句是一首小调的歌词。因 Pillicock 与上行中的 pelican 发音近似，Tom 就故意用以装疯卖傻。

75　解释不一，可能是小调末尾的副歌。

78　justly：just, truthful.　**commit not**：do not commit adultery.

79—80　proud array：ostentatious clothes.

82　servingman：either lover or servant.

83　wore gloves in my cap：在伊丽莎白时代，侍臣中时兴把情人的手套系在自己的帽子上，以示得宠。

84　act of darkness：sexual intercourse.

85　spake：spoke.

88—89　out-paramoured the Turk：had more mistresses than the Grand Turk, the Sultan, has in his harem.

89　light of ear：quick to believe any accounts of evil.

92　creaking of shoes：当时人们以穿走起路来吱吱作响的鞋为时髦。

94　plackets：openings in petticoats or skirts.　**lenders**：money-lenders.

96　suum…nonny：当时的歌曲常用一些无意义的词作副歌。suum 可能是模拟飒飒的风声。

97　Dolphin…by：可能是一首歌的歌词。

98　thou wert better：it would be better for you to be.

98—99　answer：suffer the consequences of, expose to.　**extremity**：extreme severity, i.e. the storm.

102　cat：civet cat，麝猫。身上的腺囊所分泌的物质可制香料。

103　on's：of us who.　**sophisticated**：i.e. fully clothed.

103—104　unaccommodated：without the trappings of civilization, i.e. without clothes.

105　forked：two-legged.　**lendings**：borrowed articles, things not man's own (referring to his clothes).

Come; unbutton here. *[Tearing off his clothes.*

Enter GLOUCESTER, *with a torch.*

Fool. Prithee, nuncle, be contented; 'tis a naughty night to swim in. Now a little fire in a wide field were like an old lecher's heart; a small spark, all the rest on's body cold.

Look! here comes a walking fire.

Edgar. This is the foul fiend Flibbertigibbet; he begins at curfew, and walks till the first cock; he gives the web and the pin, squinies the eye, and makes the harelip; mildews the white wheat, and hurts the poor creature of earth.

    Swithold footed thrice the old;
      He met the night-mare, and her nine-fold;
        Bid her alight,
        And her troth plight,
    And aroint thee, witch, aroint thee!

Kent. How fares your Grace?

Lear. What's he?

Kent. Who's there? What is 't you seek?

Gloucester. What are you there? Your names?

Edgar. Poor Tom; that eats the swimming frog; the toad, the tadpole, the wall-newt, and the water; that in the fury of his heart, when the foul fiend rages, eats cow-dung for sallets; swallows the old rat and the ditch-dog; drinks the green mantle of the standing pool; who is whipped from tithing to tithing, and stock-punished, and imprisoned; who hath had three suits to his back, six shirts to his body, horse to ride, and weapon to wear;

    But mice and rats and such small deer
    Have been Tom's food for seven long year.

Beware my follower. Peace, Smulkin! peace, thou

ACT III SCENE IV

107 Prithee: Pray thee (you). **naughty**: bad.

108 were: would be.

109 lecher: lustful man. **on's**: of his. **cold**: 前省略 being.

110 walking fire: 指 Gloucester 的火把。

111 Flibbertigibbet: 妖精名, 出自 Harsnett 的"A Declaration of Egregious Popish Impostures"(1603)一书(参见 Lines 135, 137, 138 以及 vi 6, 30)。

112 first cock: the first cockcrow before dawn.

112—113 the web and the pin: 白内障和针眼。

113 squinies: makes it squint.

114 white: ripening. **the poor creature of earth**: mankind.

115 Swithold: St. Withold, 为 St. Vitalis 的讹称, 能镇魔驱鬼的圣者。 **old**: wold, upland.

116 night-mare: incubus, demon of the night. **nine-fold**: nine offspring or nine attendant imps.

118 her troth plight: give her pledge (not to harm anybody).

119 aroint: begone.

121 he: i.e. Gloucester.

125 wall-newt: lizard. **water**: water-newt, 蝾螈。

127 sallets: salads.

128 ditch-dog: carcass of the dog left in the ditch. **mantle**: covering, scum.

129 tithing: hamlet (originally holding ten families). 按当时的法律, 要用鞭子驱赶流浪汉, 以迫使他返回家乡。

130 stock-punished: punished by being put in the stocks.

133 deer: animals.

135 follower: familiar spirit. **Smulkin**: 妖精名。

friend.

Gloucester. What! hath your Grace no better company?

Edgar. The prince of darkness is a gentleman; Modo he's call'd, and Mahu.

Gloucester. Our flesh and blood, my lord, is grown so vile,
140 That it doth hate what gets is.

Edgar. Poor Tom's a-cold.

Gloucester. Go in with me. My duty cannot suffer
To obey in all your daughters' hard commands:
Though their injunction be to bar my doors,
145 And let this tyrannous night take hold upon you,
Yet have I ventur'd to come seek you out
And bring you where both fire and food is ready.

Lear. First let me talk with this philosopher.
What is the cause of thunder?

150 *Kent.* Good my lord, take his offer; go into the house.

Lear. I'll take a word with this same learned Theban.
What is your study?

Edgar. How to prevent the fiend, and to kill vermin.

Lear. Let me ask you one word in private.

155 *Kent.* Importune him once more to go, my lord;
His wits begin to unsettle.

Gloucester.   Canst thou blame him?

[*Storm still.*

His daughters seek his death. Ah! that good Kent;
He said it would be thus, poor banish'd man!
Thou sayst the king grows mad. I'll tell thee, friend,
160 I am almost mad myself. I had a son,
Now outlaw'd from my blood; he sought my life,
But lately, very late; I lov'd him, friend,
No father his son dearer; true to tell thee,

[*Storm continues.*

The grief hath craz'd my wits. What a night's this!

ACT III SCENE IV

137 **prince of darkness**: Satan. **Modo**: 妖精名。
138 **Mahu**: 妖精名。
139 **flesh and blood**: offspring.
140 **gets**: begets.
142 **suffer**: allow (me).
143 **in**: in the case of.
146 **come seek**: come to seek.
148 **philosopher**: natural philosopher，以前的自然科学家，这里指 Edgar.
151 **Theban**: Thebes，人，哲人。174 行 Athenian 类似。
152 **study**: specialty, department of research.
153 **prevent**: take preventative measures against, avoid.
161 **outlaw'd ... blood**: disowned by me.
162 **late**: lately, recently.

165   I do beseech your Grace, —
Lear.   O! cry you mercy, sir.
Noble philosopher, your company.
Edgar. Tom's a-cold.
Gloucester. In, fellow, there into the hovel; keep thee warm.
Lear. Come, let's in all.
Kent.   This way, my lord.
Lear.   With him;
170   I will keep still with my philosopher.
Kent. Good my lord, soothe him; let him take the fellow.
Gloucester. Take him you on.
Kent. Sirrah, come on; go along with us.
Lear. Come, good Athenian.
Gloucester.   No words, no words; hush.
175   *Edgar.* Child Rowland to the dark tower came,
           His word was still, Fie, foh, and fum,
           I smell the blood of a British man.   [*Exeunt.*

SCENE V

A ROOM IN GLOUCESTER'S CASTLE

Enter CORNWALL *and* EDMUND.

Cornwall. I will have my revenge ere I depart his house.
Edmund. How, my lord, I may be censured, that nature thus gives way to loyalty, something fears me to think of.
Cornwall. I now perceive it was not altogether your
5   brother's evil disposition made him seek his death; but a provoking merit, set a-work by a reproveable badness inhimself.
Edmund. How malicious is my fortune, that I must

ACT III SCENE V

165 cry you mercy: beg your pardon.

170 keep still: stay always.

171 soothe: humour.

172 Take...on: Take him (Edgar) along with you.

175 Child: 对骑士候补者的称呼。　**Rowland**: Roland, 法国传说中的英雄, 法兰克王查理曼之侄。这几行可能是出自民谣和故事的引语。

176 His...still: His motto or watchword was always.

176—177 Fie...man: 童话《巨人杀手杰克》Jack, the Giant-Killer 中巨人说的话, 故意错安在英雄 Rowland 头上。

III.v

1 depart: depart from.

2—3　i.e. It rather frightens me to think how I may be judged for allowing my natural affection to give way to my sense of duty.

5 made: 前省略 that.　**his**: Gloucester's.

6—7 a provoking...in himself: a virtue apt to be provoked, that was set to work by a reprehensible wickedness in Gloucester himself.

repent to be just! This is the letter he spoke of, which approves him an intelligent party to the advantages of France. O heavens! that this treason were not, or not I the detector!

Cornwall. Go with me to the duchess.

Edmund. If the matter of this paper be certain, you have mighty business in hand.

Cornwall. True, or false, it hath made thee Earl of Gloucester. Seek out where thy father is, that he may be ready for our apprehension.

Edmund. [*Aside.*] If I find him comforting the king it will stuff his suspicion more fully. I will persever in my course of loyalty, though the conflict be sore between that and my blood.

Cornwall. I will lay trust upon thee; and thou shalt find a dearer father in my love. [*Exeunt.*

SCENE VI

A CHAMBER IN A FARMHOUSE ADJOINING THE CASTLE

Enter GLOUCESTER, LEAR, KENT, Fool,
and EDGAR.

Gloucester. Here is better than the open air; take it thankfully. I will piece out the comfort with what addition I can; I will not be long from you.

Kent. All the power of his wits has given way to his impatience. The gods reward your kindness!

[*Exit* GLOUCESTER.

Edgar. Frateretto calls me, and tells me Nero is an angler in the lake of darkness. Pray, innocent, and beware the foul fiend.

Fool. Prithee, nuncle, tell we whether a madman be a gentleman or a yeoman!

Lear. A king, a king!

ACT III SCENE VI

9　to be just: of being righteous (in revealing my father's treason).
the letter: see III.iii 10.

10　approves: proves.　**intelligent party**: person giving intelligence, spy.

11—12　were not: did not exist.　**not I**: it were not I who was.

17　that: so that.

18　our apprehension: arrest by us.

19　comforting: supporting.

20　stuff his suspicion: substantiate our suspicion of him.　**persever**: persevere.

22　blood: natural feeling as a son.

III.vi

2　piece: eke.

3　from: away from.

5　impatience: inability to endure more.　**The**: 前省略 may.

6　Frateretto: 妖精名。

6—7　Nero...darkness: A legend from Chaucer's "Monk's Tale". Nero 为古代罗马暴君。　lake of darkness 为地狱中湖。

7　innocent: simpleton, idiot (addressed to the Fool).

10　yeoman: 自耕农。

Fool. No; he's a yeoman that has a gentleman to his son; for he's a mad yeoman that sees his son a gentleman before him.

Lear. To have a thousand with red burning spits
Come hizzing in upon 'em, —

Edgar. The foul fiend bites my back.

Fool. He's mad that trusts in the tameness of a wolf, a horse's health, a boy's love, or a whore's oath.

Lear. It shall be done; I will arraign them straight.
[*To* EDGAR.] Come, sit thou here, most learned justicer;
[*To the* Fool.] Thou, sapient sir, sit here. Now, you she foxes!

Edgar. Look, where he stands and glares! wantest thou eyes at trial, madam?

Come o'er the bourn, Bessy, to me, —

Fool. Her boat hath a leak,
And she must not speak
Why she dares not come over to thee.

Edgar. The foul fiend haunts poor Tom in the voice of a nightingale. Hopdance cries in Tom's belly for two white herring. Croak not, black angel; I have no food for thee.

Kent. How do you, sir? Stand you not so amaz'd: Will you lie down and rest upon the cushions?

Lear. I'll see their trial first. Bring in their evidence.
[*To* EDGAR.] Thou robed man of justice, take thy place;
[*To the* Fool.] And thou, his yoke-fellow of equity,
Bench by his side. [*To* KENT.] You are o' the commission, Sit you too.

Edgar. Let us deal justly.

Sleepest or wakest thou, jolly shepherd?
Thy sheep be in the corn;

ACT III SCENE VI 143

12—13 to his son: for his son.

15 a thousand: i.e. devils. Lear 想象他的两个女儿在地狱里受到惩罚。

16 hizzing: hissing 的变体。

18—19 a horse's health: 马是娇气的动物,容易得病。一说是指马贩子总是夸自己的马好,信不得。

20 arraign them straight: bring them (his daughters) at once before a court for trial.

21—22 justicer: judge.

22 sapient: wise.

23 he: the fiend that Edgar pretends to see.

23—24 wantest thou eyes: do you want people to look at you? or can't you see him?

24 madam: 指想象中正在受审的 Goneril 或 Regan.

25 Come…me: 这是一首通俗歌曲的开头。后面三行则是 Fool 杜撰的。 **bourn**: 一作 burn,苏格兰语 stream.

30 Hopdance: 妖精名。

31 white: fresh. **Croak not**: Do not rumble. **black angel**: fallen angel, devil.

32 amaz'd: bewildered, dumbfounded.

34 their evidence: the witnesses against them.

35 robed: Tom 当时身上披着毯子。

36 yoke-fellow of equity: partner in justice.

37—38 Bench: sit on bench (as a judge). **o' the commission**: of the commission of peace, appointed a justice of the peace.

40—43 这是另一首歌的歌词,意思与上下文并无关联,只是 Edgar 装疯的又一表现。

41—43 i.e. Your sheep are in the cornfield, and will not come to harm if you give just one blast (of the horn) from your dainty (minikin) mouth.

41 corn: cornfield, 在英国为小麦地或燕麦地。

And for one blast of thy minikin mouth,
>Thy sheep shall take no harm.

Purr! the cat is grey.

45 *Lear.* Arraign her first; 'tis Goneril. I here take my oath before this honourable assembly, she kicked the poor king her father.

Fool. Come hither, mistress. Is your name Goneril?

Lear. She cannot deny it.

50 *Fool.* Cry you mercy, I took you for a joint-stool.

Lear. And here's another, whose warp'd looks proclaim
What store her heart is made on. Stop her there!
Arms, arms, sword, fire! Corruption in the place!
False justicer, why hast thou let her 'scape?

55 *Edgar.* Bless thy five wits!

Kent. O pity! Sir, where is the patience now
That you so oft have boasted to retain?

Edgar. [*Aside.*] My tears begin to take his part so much, They'll mar my counterfeiting.

60 *Lear.* The little dogs and all,
Tray, Blanch, and Sweet-heart, see, they bark at me.

Edgar. Tom will throw his head at them. Avaunt, you curs!

>Be thy mouth or black or white,
65 >Tooth that poisons if it bite;
>Mastiff, greyhound, mongrel grim,
>Hound or spaniel, brach or lym;
>Or bobtail tike or trundle-tail;
>Tom will make them weep and wail:
70 >For, with throwing thus my head,
>Dogs leap the hatch, and all are fled.

Do de, de, de. Sessa! Come, march to wakes and fairs and market-towns. Poor Tom, thy horn is dry.

Lear. Then let them anatomize Regan, see what breeds

ACT III SCENE VI

44 Purr：妖精名，妖精常化身为猫，或以呜呜声作猫名。 **the cat is grey**：an allusion to the proverb：'All cats are grey in the dark'.

50 Cry you mercy：Forgive me. **joint-stool**：stool made carefully by a joiner. Lear 用两只凳子当作女儿。此行为英谚。

51 another：i.e. Regan. **warp'd**：crooked, perverse.

52 store：material, stuff. **on**：of.

53 Corruption…place：Bribery in the court.

55 five wits：faculties of common sense, imagination, fantasy, estimation and memory.

58 take his part：flow in sympathy with him.

59 counterfeiting：disguise.

61 Tray, Blanch, Sweet-heart：狗名。

62 head：挂在腰间的牛角，作杯用。 **Avaunt**：Get away.

64 or…or：either…or.

67 brach：hound bitch. **lym**：a kind of bloodhound.

68 bobtail tike：short-tailed cur. **trundle-tail**：long-tailed.

71 leap the hatch：make a hurried exit. hatch 为分上下两部分的门的下半扇。

72 Do de…Sessa：see III.iv 56 and 97. **wakes**：church festivals.

73 horn：a beggar's drinking horn.

74 anatomize：dissect.

75 about her heart. Is there any cause in nature that makes these hard hearts? [*To* EDGAR.] You, sir, I entertain you for one of my hundred; only I do not like the fashion of your garments: you will say, they are Persian attire; but let them be changed.

80 *Kent.* Now, good my lord, lie here and rest awhile.

Lear. Make no noise, make no noise; draw the curtains: so, so, so. We'll go to supper i' the morning: so, so, so.

Fool. And I'll go to bed at noon.

Re-enter GLOUCESTER.

Gloucester. Come hither, friend: where is the king my
85 master?

Kent. Here, sir; but trouble him not, his wits are gone.

Gloucester. Good friend, I prithee, take him in thy arms;
I have o'erheard a plot of death upon him.
There is a litter ready; lay him in 't.
90 And drive toward Dover, friend, where thou shalt meet
Both welcome and protection. Take up thy master:
If thou shouldst dally half an hour, his life,
With thine, and all that offer to defend him,
Stand in assured loss. Take up, take up;
95 And follow me, that will to some provision
Give thee quick conduct.

Kent.   Oppress'd nature sleeps:
This rest might yet have balm'd thy broken sinews,
Which, if convenience will not allow,
Stand in hard cure. — [*To the* Fool.] Come, help to bear thy master;
Thou must not stay behind.

ACT III SCENE VI

77 entertain: take into my service, engage. **hundred**: i.e., hundred knights.

79 Persian: 波斯服饰以精美闻名,但这里是反话。

81—82 curtains: 指 Lear 想象中自己床周围的帐子。

83 bed: 又指坟墓。此行以后,Fool 不再说话,下场后不再出现。

88 upon: against.

89 litter: 一种无顶篷的轿子,此处为马驮的担架。

90 drive: carry.

92 dally: delay.

93 offer: dare, venture.

94 Stand in assured loss: Are certain to be lost.

95 that: who. **provision**: food, supplies.

96 conduct(n.): guidance.

97 balm'd: healed like a balm. **broken sinews**: racked nerves.

98 convenience: means for promoting comfort.

99 Stand…cure: Can hardly be cured.

Gloucester. Come, come, away.
  [*Exeunt* KENT, GLOUCESTER,
  and the Fool, *bearing away* LEAR.

Edgar. When we our betters see bearing our woes,
  We scarcely think our miseries our foes.
  Who alone suffers suffers most i' the mind,
  Leaving free things and happy shows behind;
  But then the mind much sufferance doth o'er-skip,
  When grief hath mates, and bearing fellowship.
  How light and portable my pain seems now,
  When that which makes me bend makes the king bow;
  He childed as I father'd! Tom, away!
  Mark the high noises, and thyself bewray
  When false opinion, whose wrong thought defiles thee,
  In thy just proof repeals and reconciles thee.
  What will hap more to-night, safe 'scape the king!
  Lurk, lurk. [*Exit.*

SCENE VII

A ROOM IN GLOUCESTERS CASTLE

Enter CORNWALL, REGAN, GONERIL,
EDMUND, *and Servants.*

Cornwall. Post speedily to my lord your husband; show him this letter: the army of France is landed. Seek out the traitor Gloucester.
  [*Exeunt some of the* Servants.

Regan. Hang him instantly.

Goneril. Pluck out his eyes.

Cornwall. Leave him to my displeasure. Edmund, keep you our sister company: the revenges we are bound to take upon your traitorous father are not fit for your beholding. Advise the duke, where you are going, to

ACT III SCENE VII

101 our woes: the same trouble as we have.

103 Who: Whoever.

104 free: carefree, free from distress. **shows**: sights.

105 sufferance: suffering. **o'er-skip**: pass over without notice, ignore.

106 mates: companions — i.e. other people to share grief. **bearing**: having.

107 portable: easy to bear.

109 childed as I father'd: provided with children as I provided with father.

110 high noises: rumours of great events, disturbances in high quarters. **thyself bewray**: reveal who you really are.

111 When: i.e. only when. **false opinion**: wrong suspicion (felt about you).

112 In thy just proof: upon proof of your integrity. **repeals**: repeals the sentence of outlawry. **reconciles**: reconciles you to your father.

113 What … hap: Whatever happens. **safe … the king**: may the king escape in safety.

114 Lurk: hide yourself, lie low.

III. vii

1 这是对 Goneril 说的。 **Post**: hasten.

2 is landed: has landed.

7 bound: ①prepared; ②obliged.

8—9 for your beholding: for you to see.

10   a most festinate preparation; we are bound to the
like. Our posts shall be swift and intelligent betwixt
us. Farewell, dear sister; farewell, my Lord of
Gloucester.

Enter OSWALD.

How now? Where's the king?
15 *Oswald*. My Lord of Gloucester hath convey'd him hence;
Some five or six and thirty of his knights,
Hot questrists after him, met him at gate;
Who, with some other of the lord's dependants,
Are gone with him toward Dover, where they boast
20 To have well-armed friends.
Cornwall.   Get horses for your mistress.
Goneril. Farewell, sweet lord, and sister.
Cornwall. Edmund, farewell.
                [*Exeunt* GONERIL, EDMUND, and OSWALD.
                Go seek the traitor Gloucester,
Pinion him like a thief, bring him before us.
                [*Exeunt other* Servants.
Though well we may not pass upon his life
25 Without the form of justice, yet our power
Shall do a courtesy to our wrath, which men
May blame but not control. Who's there? The traitor?

Re-enter Servants, *with* GLOUCESTER.

Regan. Ingrateful fox! 'tis he.
Cornwall. Bind fast his corky arms.
30 *Gloucester*. What mean your Graces? Good my friends, consider
You are my guests; do me no foul play, friends.
Cornwall. Bind him, I say.   [Servants *bind him*.
Regan.   Hard, hard. O filthy traitor!

10　festinate: speedy.

10—11　bound...like: ready to do the same.

11　posts: speedy messengers on horseback.　　**intelligent**: carry information efficiently.

12—13　Lord of Gloucester: 指 Edmund（见 III.v 16—17）。

17　questrists: seekers.

23　Pinion: cut a wing of, 转义 confine, detain.

24　pass: pass the death sentence.

26　do a courtesy to: bow before, give way to.

27　control: hinder.

29　corky: withered, like dry cork.

32　filthy: odious.

Gloucester. Unmerciful lady as you are, I'm none.
Cornwall. To this chair bind him. Villain, thou shalt
    find — [REGAN *plucks his beard.*
Gloucester. By the kind gods, 'tis most ignobly done
  To pluck me by the beard.
Regan. So white, and such a traitor!
Gloucester.   Naughty lady,
  These hairs, which thou dost ravish from my chin,
  Will quicken, and accuse thee: I am your host:
  With robbers' hands my hospitable favours
  You should not ruffle thus. What will you do?
Cornwall. Come, sir, what letters had you late from France?
Regan. Be simple-answer'd, for we know the truth.
Cornwall. And what confederacy have you with the traitors
  Late footed in the kingdom?
Regan. To whose hands have you sent the lunatic king?
  Speak.
Gloucester. I have a letter guessingly set down,
  Which came from one that's of a neutral heart,
  And not from one oppos'd.
Cornwall.   Cunning.
Regan.   And false
Cornwall. Where hast thou sent the king?
Gloucester.   To Dover.
Regan. Wherefore to Dover? Wast thou not charg'd at peril —
Cornwall. Wherefore to Dover? Let him answer that.
Gloucester. I am tied to the stake, and I must stand the course.
Regan. Wherefore to Dover?
Gloucester. Because I would not see thy cruel nails
  Pluck out his poor old eyes; nor thy fierce sister

ACT III SCENE VII

33 none: i.e. not a traitor.

37 Naughty: wicked. 在伊丽莎白时代,这个词的词义远比现在强烈。

38 ravish: pull out.

39 quicken: come to life.

40 hospitable favours: features of a host.

41 ruffle: treat violently, abuse.

42 late: lately.

43 Be simple-answer'd: Answer straightforwardly.

44 confederacy: conspiracy.

45 footed: gained a footing.

48 guessingly set down: written from conjecture, not knowledge.

52 charg'd at peril: ordered on peril of death.

54 tied to the stake: like a bear. **course**: a relay of dogs set on a baited bear. 斗熊为当时一种残忍的游戏,一次次地纵狗去咬一头拴在柱子上的熊。

In his anointed flesh stick boarish fangs.
The sea, with such a storm as his bare head
60 In hell-black night endur'd, would have buoy'd up,
And quench'd the stelled fires;
Yet, poor old heart, he holp the heavens to rain.
If wolves had at thy gate howl'd that dern time,
Thou shouldst have said, 'Good porter, turn the key,'
65 All cruels else subscrib'd: but I shall see
The winged vengeance overtake such children.

Cornwall. See 't shalt thou never. Fellows, hold the chair.
Upon these eyes of thine I'll set my foot.

Gloucester. He that will think to live till he be old,
70 Give me some help! O cruel! O ye gods!
[GLOUCESTER'S *eye put out*.

Regan. One side will mock another; the other too.

Cornwall. If you see vengeance. —

First Servant. Hold your hand, my lord:
I have serv'd you ever since I was a child,
But better service have I never done you
75 Than now to bid you hold.

Regan. How now, you dog!

First Servant. If you did wear a beard upon your chin,
I'd shake it on this quarrel.

Regan. What do you mean?

Cornwall. My villain! [*Draws.*

First Servant. Nay then, come on, and take the chance of anger. [*Draws. They fight.*
[CORNWALL *is wounded*.

80 *Regan.* Give me thy sword. A peasant stand up thus!
[*Takes a sword, and runs at him behind.*

First Servant. O! I am slain. My lord, you have one eye left.

58　anointed: consecrated with holy oil. 国王在加冕时要行涂油礼,以表示"君权神授"。

60　buoy'd up: risen up, like a buoy.

61　stelled fires: fixed stars.

62　holp: helped.

63　dern: dire, dreadful.

64　turn the key: i.e. open the door and let them in.

65　All cruels else subscrib'd: All other cruel things (except the storm) would be admitted.

66　winged vengeance: angels of vengeance.

69　will think: hopes.

71　One…another: i.e. The side of Gloucester's face which still has an eye will mock the other.　**the other too**: the other eye too.

72　Hold: stop.

75　How now: What is this?

76　此行说,如果你是男人。

77　shake it: i.e. defy you (to fight).

78　villain: serf, servant.

79　take…anger: take the chance result where anger, not skill, directs the weapon.

80　stand up: rise up.

To see some mischief on him. O! [*Dies*.

Cornwall. Lest it see more, prevent it. Out, vile jelly!
Where is thy lustre now?

Gloucester. All dark and comfortless. Where's my son
Edmund?
Edmund, enkindle all the sparks of nature
To quit this horrid act.

Regan. Out, treacherous villain!
Thou call'st on him that hates thee; it was he
That made the overture of thy treasons to us,
Who is too good to pity thee.

Gloucester. O my follies! Then Edgar was abus'd.
Kind gods, forgive me that, and prosper him!

Regan. Go thrust him out at gates, and let him smell
His way to Dover. [*Exit one with* GLOUCESTER.]
How is't, my lord? How look you?

Cornwall. I have receiv'd a hurt. Follow me, lady.
Turn out that eyeless villain; throw this slave
Upon the dunghill. Regan, I bleed apace:
Untimely comes this hurt. Give me your arm.
[*Exit* CORNWALL, *led by* REGAN.

Second Servant. I'll never care what wickedness I do
If this man come to good.

Third Servant. If she live long,
And, in the end, meet the old course of death,
Women will all turn monsters.

Second Servant. Let's follow the old earl, and get the
Bedlam
To lead him where he would: his roguish madness
Allows itself to any thing.

Third Servant. Go thou; I'll fetch some flax, and
whites of eggs,
To apply to his bleeding face. Now, heaven help him!
[*Exeunt severally*.

ACT III SCENE VII

82 **mischief**: injury, harm.　**him**: 指 Cornwall.
83 **prevent it**: let me prevent it.　**jelly**: 指眼珠。
86 **nature**: filial feeling.
87 **quit**: requite, avenge.　**Out**: 呸(表示愤怒或憎恶的感叹词)。
89 **overture**: disclosure.
90 **Who**: 与上行 That 同位。
91 **abus'd**: wronged.
92 **prosper**(v.t.): cause … to prosper.
94 **How look you?**: How are things with you?
101 **old**: usual, natural.
103 **Bedlam**: Beggar, 指 Edgar.
104 **would**: wish to be led.

104—105 **his roguish … any thing**: The fact that he is a mad vagrant allows him to do anything with impunity.

ACT IV

SCENE I

THE HEATH

Enter EDGAR.

Edgar. Yet better thus, and known to be contemn'd,
Than still contemn'd and flatter'd. To be worst,
The lowest and most dejected thing of fortune,
Stands still in esperance, lives not in fear:
5 The lamentable change is from the best;
The worst returns to laughter. Welcome, then,
Thou unsubstantial air that I embrace:
The wretch that thou hast blown unto the worst
Owes nothing to thy blasts. But who comes here?

Enter GLOUCESTER, *led by an* Old Man.

10 My father, poorly led? World, world, O world!
But that thy strange mutations make us hate thee,
Life would not yield to age.
Old Man.   O my good lord!
I have been your tenant, and your father's tenant,
These fourscore years.
15 *Gloucester.* Away, get thee away; good friend, be gone;
Thy comforts can do me no good at all;
Thee they may hurt.
Old Man.   You cannot see your way.
Gloucester. I have no way, and therefore want no eyes;
I stumbled when I say. Full oft 'tis seen,
20 Our means secure us, and our mere defects
Prove our commodities. Ah! dear son Edgar,
The food of thy abused father's wrath;
Might I but live to see thee in my touch,

IV. i

1 **Yet better thus**: it is better to be thus. **known ... contemn'd**: known to yourself to be despised.

2 **still**: at the same time.

3 **most ... fortune**: the thing cast down lowest by fortune. **of**: at the hands of.

4 **esperance**: hope.

6 **returns to laughter**: may yet see oneself happy again.

9 **Owes nothing to**: has paid his full debt to, and has therefore nothing more to fear from.

10 **poorly led**: led by a poor man.

11 **But that**: If it were not that. **thy**: 指 world's.

12 **Life ... age**: We should not be reconciled to old age and ultimate death.

16 **comforts**: attempts to help.

20 **Our means ... us**: Our resources make us feel secure and therefore grow careless.

20—21 **our mere ... commodities**: it is precisely our weaknesses that turn out to be advantages.

22 **food**: object. **abused**: deceived, misled.

23 **in**: by means of.

I'd say I had eyes again.

Old Man. How now! who's there?

Edgar. [*Aside.*] O gods! Who is 't can say, 'I am at the worst'?

I am worse than e'er I was.

Old Man. 'Tis poor mad Tom.

Edgar. [*Aside.*] And worse I may be yet; the worst is not,

So long as we can say, 'This is the worst.'

Old Man. Fellow, where goest?

Gloucester. Is it a beggar-man?

Old Man. Madman and beggar too.

Gloucester. He has some reason, else he could not beg.
I' the last night's storm I such a fellow saw,
Which made me think a man a worm: my son
Came then into my mind; and yet my mind
Was then scarce friends with him: I have heard more since.
As flies to wanton boys, are we to the gods;
They kill us for their sport.

Edgar. [*Aside.*] How should this be?
Bad is the trade that must play fool to sorrow,
Angering itself and others. — [*To* GLOUCESTER.]
Bless thee, master!

Gloucester. Is that the naked fellow?

Old Man. Ay, my lord.

Gloucester. Then, prithee, get thee gone. If, for my sake,
Thou wilt o'ertake us, hence a mile or twain,
I' the way toward Dover, do it for ancient love;
And bring some covering for this naked soul
Who I'll entreat to lead me.

Old Man. Alack, sir! he is mad.

Gloucester. 'Tis the times' plague, when madmen lead

ACT IV SCENE I

24 I'd say … again: i. e. It would be as good as recovering my sight.

27 the worst is not: i. e. we have not reached the worst.

29 where goest: where are you going?

31 He has some reason: He's not quite mad.　**reason**: ability to reason.

35 scarce friends with him: scarcely well disposed towards him.　**more**: viz.

36 wanton: playful.

37 How should this be?: What has happened to make this come about.

38 i. e. it's a bad job when we have to play fool in the presence of sorrow (as I am now doing).

39 Angering: Distressing.

41 get thee gone: get on your way.

42 o'ertake: catch up with.　**twain**: two.

43 ancient love: i. e. the sort of love that used to exist between men.

44 covering: clothing.

46 times' plague: 时代病。

the blind.
Do as I bid thee, or rather do thy pleasure;
Above the rest, be gone.

Old Man. I'll bring him the best 'parel that I have,
50   Come on 't what will.   [*Exit*.

Gloucester. Sirrah, naked fellow, —

Edgar. Poor Tom's a-cold. [*Aside*.] I cannot daub it further.

Gloucester. Come hither, fellow.

Edgar. [*Aside*.] And yet I must. Bless thy sweet eyes, they bleed.

55   *Gloucester*. Know'st thou the way to Dover?

Edgar. Both stile and gate, horse-way and footpath. Poor Tom hath been scared out of his good wits: bless thee, good man's son, from the foul fiend! Five fiends have been in poor Tom at once; of lust, as Obidicut;
60   Hobbididance, prince of dumbness; Mahu, of stealing; Modo, of murder; and Flibbertigibbet, of mopping and mowing; who since possesses chambermaids and waiting-women. So, bless thee, master!

Gloucester. Here, take this purse, thou whom the heavens' plagues
65   Have humbled to all strokes: that I am wretched
Makes thee the happier: heavens, deal so still!
Let the superfluous and lust-dieted man,
That slaves your ordinance, that will not see
Because he doth nor feel, feel your power quickly;
70   So distribution should undo excess,
And each man have enough. Dost thou know Dover?

Edgar. Ay, master.

Gloucester. There is a cliff, whose high and bending head
Looks fearfully in the confined deep;
75   Bring me but to the very brim of it,

ACT IV SCENE I

47 do thy pleasure: do as you wish.

48 Above the rest: Above all things.

49 'parel: apparel.

50 Come…will: whatever the consequences may be. **on 't**: of it.

52 daub it: dissemble, pretend. daub 原意为"刷石灰",转意"糊弄"。

56 stile: ①供行人爬越墙篱的木头梯级; ② = turnstile,绕杆。 **gate**: 木栅门。英国乡间小路上多有这些东西,目的在挡住牛羊,而让行人仍可通过。

57—58 bless thee…from: God preserve thee from.

59—61 Obidicut…Flibbertigibbet: 这五个妖精名都出自 Harsenett,有时拼法略有不同。

62 mopping and mowing: grimacing, making faces. **since**: from that time on.

65 humbled to: humbled into bearing. **strokes**: strokes of fortune, misfortunes. **that**: the fact that.

66 happier: less wretched. **heavens…still**: O Heavens, deal always this way (with mortlas).

67 superfluous: having more than he needs. **lust-dieted**: whose lusts are surfeited.

68 slaves your ordinance: makes your commands his slaves, i.e., for his own purposes.

69 第一个 feel: feel sympathy for others.

70 undo: do away with.

71 have: 多数,似乎主语为 all men.

73 bending: overhanging, beetling.

74 fearfully: frighteningly. **in**: into. **the confined deep**: the sea bounded by the cliffs.

And I'll repair the misery thou dost bear
With something rich about me; from that place
I shall no leading need.
Edgar.   Give me thy arm:
Poor Tom shall lead thee.   [*Exeunt*.

SCENE II

BEFORE THE DUKE OF ALBANY'S PALACE

Enter GONERIL *and* EDMUND.

Goneril. Welcome, my lord; I marvel our mild husband
Not met us on the way. [*Enter* OSWALD.] Now,
where's your master?
Oswald. Madam, within; but never man so chang'd.
I told him of the army that was landed;
5 He smil'd at it: I told him you were coming;
His answer was, 'The worse': of Gloucester's treachery,
And of the loyal service of his son,
When I inform'd him, then he call'd me sot,
And told me I had turn'd the wrong side out:
10 What most he should dislike seems pleasant to him;
What like, offensive.
Goneril.[*To* EDMUND.] Then, shall you go no further.
It is the cowish terror of his spirit
That dares not undertake; he'll not feel wrongs
Which tie him to an answer. Our wishes on the way
15 May prove effects. Back, Edmund, to my brother;
Hasten his musters and conduct his powers:
I must change arms at home, and give the distaff
Into my husband's hands. This trusty servant
Shall pass between us; ere long you are like to hear,
20 If you dare venture in your own behalf,
A mistress's command. Wear this; spare speech;

76 repair: redress, alleviate.

IV. ii

1 Welcome: i.e. to our house.　**mild**: 反应。

2 Not met: Did not meet.　**on the way**: i.e., from Gloucester's castle.

3 within: indoors.

6 The worse: So much the worse.

7 his son: Gloucester's son, Edmund.

8 sot: fool.

9 turn'd … out: got things inside out, inverted right and wrong.

11 What like, offensive: What he should like seems offensive.

12 cowish: cowardly.

13 undertake(v.i.): make an attempt, embark on a venture.

13—14 he'll … answer: he will ignore such insults as require in honour to be answered.

14—15 Our wishes … May prove effects: What we wished for on our journey here may be realized (i.e. that you should replace him).

15 brother: i.e. 妹夫 Cornwall.

16 musters: assembling of forces.　**conduct his powers**: lead his army.

17 change arms: i.e. take the sword in exchange (for the distaff). **distaff**: 纺线杆，象征妇女的家务活。

19 pass: carry messages.　**like**: likely.

20 in your own behalf: on your own part.

[Giving a favour.
Decline your head: this kiss, if it durst speak,
Would stretch thy spirits up into the air.
Conceive, and fare thee well.

25 *Edmund.* Yours in the ranks of death.
Goneril. My most dear Gloucester!
[Exit EDMUND.

O! the difference of man and man!
To thee a woman's services are due:
My fool usurps my bed.
Oswald. Madam, here comes my lord. *[Exit.*

Enter ALBANY.

Goneril. I have been worth the whistle.
Albany. O Goneril!
30 You are not worth the dust which the rude wind
Blows in your face. I fear your disposition
That nature, which contemns its origin,
Cannot be border'd certain in itself;
She that herself will sliver and disbranch
35 From her material sap, perforce must wither
And come to deadly use.
Goneril. No more; the text is foolish.
Albany. Wisdom and goodness to the vile seem vile;
Filths savour but themselves. What have you done?
40 Tigers, not daughters, what have you perform'd?
A father, and a gracious aged man,
Whose reverence the head-lugg'd bear would lick,
Most barbarous, most degenerate! have you madded.
Could my good brother suffer you to do it?
45 A man, a prince, by him so benefited!
If that the heavens do not their visible spirits
Send quickly down to tame these vile offences,
It will come,

ACT IV SCENE II   167

s.d.favour：信物。

22 Decline：bend (for a kiss). **durst**：dared to.

24 Conceive：Take my meaning.

25 ranks of death：①dangerous enterprise；②practice of sexual orgasm.

26 of：between.

28 My fool：My husband who is a fool.

29 worth the whistle：worth being welcomed home (cf. English proverb 'It's a poor dog that is not worth the whistling').

30 rude：rough.

31 fear：fear for (what your disposition may lead to).

32 contemns：despises.

33 border'd certain：kept safely within bounds.

34 sliver and disbranch：tear off (as a twig from a branch).

35 material：forming the substance of a thing, essential.

36 come to deadly use：be used as dead wood (for burning).

37 text：subject of your sermon.

39 Filths…but themselves：Filthy creatures enjoy only things that are filthy.

42   i. e. whose grey hairs even a beast would respect. **head-lugg'd**：pulled about by the head, i.e. sulky.

43 madded：become mad.

44 suffer：allow.

45 him：i.e. Lear.

46 If that：If. **visible**：in visible form.

47 offences：offenders.

48 It：The sending of punishment.

Humanity must perforce prey on itself,
50 Like monsters of the deep.
   Goneril.   Milk-liver'd man!
That bear'st a cheek for blows, a head for wrongs;
Who hast not in thy brows an eye discerning
Thine honour from thy suffering; that not knows'st
Fools do those villains pity who are punish'd
55 Ere they have done their mischief. Where's thy drum?
France spreads his banners in our noiseless land,
With plumed helm thy state begins to threat,
Whilst thou, a moral fool, sitt'st still, and criest
'Alack! why does he so?'
   Albany.   See thyself, devil!
60 Proper deformity seems not in the fiend
So horrid as in woman.
   Goneril.   O vain fool!
   Albany. Thou changed and self-cover'd thing, for shame,
Be-monster not thy feature. Were't my fitness
To let these hands obey my blood,
65 They are apt enough to dislocate and tear
Thy flesh and bones; howe'er thou art a fiend,
A woman's shape doth shield thee.
   Goneril. Marry, your manhood. — Mew!

Enter a Messenger.

   Albany. What news?
70   *Messenger.* O! my good lord, the Duke of Cornwall's dead;
Slain by his servant, going to put out
The other eye of Gloucester.
   Albany.   Gloucester's eyes!
   Messenger. A servant that he bred, thrill'd with remorse,

ACT IV SCENE II

50 deep: sea. **Milk-liver'd**: white-livered, cowardly.

51 i.e. you are the sort of man to 'turn the other cheek'(《圣经·新约·马太福音》第 5 章第 39 节). **for**: waiting for.

52—53 brows: forehead. **discerning … suffering**: able to distinguish between an insult to your honour and what you should tolerate.

54—55 That only fools pity villains because they will be punished, even before they ….

56 noiseless: with no sound of drums, hence peaceful.

57 Begins to threaten your kingdom with plumed helmet (soldiers).

58 moral: moralizing.

60—61 Proper … woman: Deformity, that is proper in the devil, shows itself more horrible in a woman.

62 changed: transformed (into a monster). **self-cover'd**: who conceals her real self.

63 Be-monster: make monstrous. **feature**: appearance. **Were't my fitness**: If it were fitting for me.

64 blood: impulse.

65 apt: ready.

66 howe'er: although.

68 Marry: By the Virgin Mary. **Mew!**: 呸(表示轻蔑和嘲弄的感叹词)。

71 going: when Cornwall was going.

73 bred: kept. **thrill'd**: moved. **with**: by. **remorse**: pity.

Oppos'd against the act, bending his sword
To his great master; who, thereat enrag'd,
Flew on him, and amongst them fell'd him dead;
But now without that harmful stroke, which since
Hath pluck'd him after.

Albany. This shows you are above,
You justicers, that these our nether crimes
So speedily can venge! But, O poor Gloucester!
Lost he his other eye?

Messenger. Both, both, my lord.
This letter, madam, craves a speedy answer;
'Tis from your sister.

Goneril. [*Aside.*] One way I like this well;
But being widow, and my Gloucester with her,
May all the building in my fancy pluck
Upon my hateful life; another way,
This news is not so tart. [*To* Messenger.] I'll read
and answer. [*Exit.*

Albany. Where was his son when they did take his eyes?

Messenger. Come with my lady hither.

Albany. He is not here.

Messenger. No, my good lord; I met him back again.

Albany. Knows he the wickedness?

Messenger. Ay, my good lord; 'twas he inform'd against him,
And quit the house on purpose that their punishment
Might have the freer course.

Albany. Gloucester, I live
To thank thee for the love thou show'dst the king,
And to revenge thine eyes. Come hither, friend;
Tell me what more thou knowest. [*Exeunt.*

ACT IV SCENE II

74 Oppos'd: opposed himself.　**bending**: directing.

75 To: Against.

76 amongst them fell'd: among Cornwall and his other servants they felled.

78 pluck'd him after: taken Cornwall away (to death).

79 justicers: judges.　**nether**: committed on earth (the lower world as opposed to heaven).

80 venge: take vengeance on, punish.

84 i. e. the fact that Regan is a widow and Gloucester (Edmund), whom I desire, is with her.

85—86 i. e. may pull down all my fine schemes and so make my life hateful to me.

86 another way: 指 Cornwall 之死使 Edmund 有可能成为英军的统帅。

87 tart: bitter.

89 my lady: i.e. Regan.

90 back: on his way back.

92 inform'd: 前省略 who.

SCENE III

THE FRENCH CAMP, NEAR DOVER

Enter KENT *and a* Gentleman.

Kent. Why the King of France is so suddenly gone back know you the reason?

Gentleman. Something he left imperfect in the state, which since his coming forth is thought of; which imports to the kingdom so much fear and danger, that his personal return was most required and necessary.

Kent. Who hath he left behind him general?

Gentleman. The Marshal of France, Monsieur la Far.

Kent. Did your letters pierce the queen to any demonstration of grief?

Gentleman. Ay, sir; she took them, read them in my presence;
And now and then an ample tear trill'd down
Her delicate cheek; it seem'd she was a queen
Over her passion; who, most rebel-like,
Sought to be king o'er her.

Kent.   O! then it mov'd her.

Gentleman. Not to a rage; patience and sorrow strove
Who should express her goodliest. You have seen
Sunshine and rain at once; her smiles and tears
Were like a better way; those happy smilets
That play'd on her ripe lip seem'd not to know
What guests were in her eyes; which parted thence,
As pearls from diamonds dropp'd. In brief,
Sorrow would be a rarity most belov'd,
If all could so become it.

Kent.   Made she no verbal question?

Gentleman. Faith, once or twice she heav'd the name of 'father'

IV. iii 此场在 1623 年对折本中整个被删去。

    3 **imperfect**: undone.

    5 **imports**: portents, carries with it.

    7 **general**: as general.

    9 **letters**: letter, 当时一封信有时称 letters. **pierce**: move, excite. **the queen**: i.e. Cordelia, Queen of France.

    12 **ample**: large. **trill'd**: trickled.

    14 **Over**: in control of. **passion**: emotion. **who**: which.

    17 **Who…goodliest**: as to which should suit her best.

    18 **at once**: together.

    19 **like a better way**: like that (sunshine and rain together), but after a better fashion (even more beautiful). **smilets**: little smiles.

    21 **which**: the guests, i.e. tears.

    22 **diamonds**: her eyes.

    23 **rarity**: precious thing.

    24 **If … it**: If all persons were as attractive in sorrow as she. **Made…question?**: Didn't she say anything? **question**: speech.

    25 **Faith**: By my faith. **heav'd**: breathed out with difficulty.

Pantingly forth, as if it press'd her heart;
Cried, 'Sisters! sisters! Shame of ladies! sisters!
Kent! father! sisters! What, i' the storm? i' the night?
Let pity not be believed!' There she shook
30　The holy water from her heavenly eyes,
And clamour-moisten'd, then away she started
To deal with grief alone.

Kent.　　　　　　　　It is the stars,
The stars above us, govern our conditions;
Else one self mate and make could not beget
35　Such different issues. You spoke not with her since?
Gentleman. No.
Kent. Was this before the king return'd?
Gentleman.　　　　　　　　No, since.
Kent. Well, sir, the poor distress'd Lear's i'the town,
Who sometime, in his better tune, remembers
40　What we are come about, and by no means
Will yield to see his daughter.
Gentleman.　　　　　　　Why, good sir?
Kent. A sovereign shame so elbows him: his own unkindness,
That stripp'd her from his benediction, turn'd her
To foreign casualties, gave her dear rights
45　To his dog-herated daughters, — these things sting
His mind so venomously that burning shame
Detains him from Cordelia.
Gentleman.　　　　　　　Alack! poor gentleman.
Kent. Of Albany's and Cornwall's powers you heard not?
Gentleman. 'Tis so, they are afoot.
50　*Kent.* Well, sir, I'll bring you to our master Lear,
And leave you to attend him. Some dear cause
Will in concealment wrap me up awhile;

ACT IV SCENE III

29 believed: believed to exist. **There**: At this point.

31 clamour-moisten'd: having her outcry of grief calmed by a flood of tears. **started**: moved suddenly.

33 conditions: characters.

34 Else: otherwise. **one self mate and make**: the same husband and wife.

37 the king (of France). **since**: after that.

39 sometime: sometimes. **better tune**: saner moments.

41 yield: consent.

42 sovereign: overruling. **elbows him**: pushes him away (from her).

43 turn'd: turned out.

44 foreign casualties: the chances of life abroad. **dear**: important.

45 dog-hearted: cruel.

47 Detains him: Keeps him away.

48 powers: forces.

49 'Tis so: It is true that. **afoot**: on the march.

51 dear cause: important reason.

When I am known aright, you shall not grieve
Lending me this acquaintance. I pray you, go
55 Along with me. [*Exeunt*.

SCENE IV

THE SAME. A TENT

Enter with drun and colours, CORDELIA,
Doctor, *and* Soldiers.

Cordelia. Alack! 'tis he; why, he was met even now
As mad as the vex'd sea; singing aloud;
Crown'd with rank fumiter and furrow weeds,
With burdocks, hemlock, nettles, cuckoo-flowers,
5 Darnel, and all the idle weeds that grow
In our sustaining corn. A century send forth;
Search every acre in the high-grown field,
And bring him to our eye. [*Exit an* Officer.
What can man's wisdom
In the restoring his bereaved sense?
10 He that helps him take all my outward worth.
Physician. There is means, madam;
Our foster-nurse of nature is repose,
The which he lacks; that to provoke in him,
Are many simples operative, whose power
15 Will close the eye of anguish.
Cordelia. All bless'd secrets,
All you unpublish'd virtues of the earth,
Spring with my tears! be aidant and remediate
In the good man's distress! Seek, seek for him,
Lest his ungovern'd rage dissolve the life
20 That wants the means to lead it.

Enter a Messenger.

Messenger. News, madam;
The British powers are marching hitherward.

53 aright: i.e., as Kent. **grieve**: repent.

54 Lending…acquaintance: for having made my acquaintance.

IV. iv

1 even now: just now.

2 vex'd: turbulent, stirred up by winds.

3 rank(adj.): luxuriant. **fumiter**: fumitory,紫堇。 **furrow weeds**: weeds which grow in ploughed land,田畦草。

4 burdocks:白酸模草。 **hemlock**:毒芹。 **nettles**:荨麻。 **cuckoo-flowers**:碎米荠。

5 Darnel:毒麦。 **idle**: worthless.

6 sustaining corn: life-giving wheat. **century**: a hundred men.

8 can: can do.

9 restoring: restoring of. 在莎士比亚时代,英语正处于从中世纪英语向现代英语转变的过渡时期。动名词的这种用法也是当时语法的特点之一。 **bereaved**: lost.

10 helps: heals. **outward worth**: worldly possessions.

12 Our…nature: The foster-nurse of our nature. 养母,奶妈。

13 The which: Which (repose). 按当时的语法,关系代词 which 前若有多个名词需要作出选择时,往往在 which 前加 the. **that to provoke**: in order to induce that (repose).

14 simples operative: effective (medicinal) herbs.

16 unpublish'd virtues: unknown healing powers.

17 Spring with: Spring up watered by. **aidant and remediate**: helpful and remedial.

19 rage: frenzy.

20 wants the means: i.e. lacks the power of reason.

21 hitherward: in this direction.

Cordelia. 'Tis known before; our preparation stands
In expectation of them. O dear father!
It is thy business that I go about;
Therefore great France
My mourning and important tears hath pitied.
No blown ambition doth our arms incite,
But love, dear love, and our ag'd father's right,
Soon may I hear and see him! [*Exeunt.*

SCENE V

A ROOM IN GLOUCESTER'S CASTLE

Enter REGAND *and* OSWALD.

Regan. But are my brother's powers set forth?
Oswald. Ay, madam.
Regan. Himself in person there
Oswald. Madam, with much ado:
Your sister is the better soldier.
Regan. Lord Edmund spake not with your lord at home?
Oswald. No, madam.
Regan. What might import my sister's letter to him?
Oswald. I know not, lady.
Regan. Faith, he is posted hence on serious matter.
It was great ignorance, Gloucester's eyes being out,
To let him live; where he arrives he moves
All hearts against us. Edmund, I think, is gone,
In pity of his misery, to dispatch
His nighted life; moreover, to descry
The strength o' the enemy.
Oswald. I must needs after him, madam, with my letter.
Regan. Our troops set forth to-morrow; stay with us,
The ways are dangerous.

ACT IV SCENE V

22 **before**: already. **preparation**: troops in readiness.
24 **business**: cause.
25 **France**: the king of France (Cordella's husband).
26 **important**: importunate, urgent.
27 **blown**: pretentions, puffed up.

IV. v

1 **brother's**: brother-in-law's.
2 **with much ado**: after much persuasion.
4 **spake**: spoke.
6 **What ... him**: What message could my sister's letter bring to him?
8 **posted**: gone with haste.
9 **ignorance**: folly.
10 **where**: wherever.
12 **dispatch**: finish.
13 **nighted**: darkened, blinded. **descry**: reconnoitre.
15 **must needs after**: must follow.

Oswald. I may not, madam;
My lady charg'd my duty in this business.
Regan. Why should she write to Edmund? Might not you
Transport her purposes by word? Belike,
Something — I know not what. I'll love thee much,
Let me unseal the letter.
Oswald. Madam, I had rather —
Regan. I know your lady does not love her husband;
I am sure of that: and at her late being here
She gave strange œilliades and most speaking looks
To noble Edmund. I know you are of her bosom.
Oswald. I, madam!
Regan. I speak in understanding; you are, I know't;
Therefore I do advise you, take this note:
My lord is dead; Edmund and I have talk'd,
And more convenient is he for my hand
Than for your lady's. You may gather more.
If you do find him, pray you, give him this,
And when your mistress hears thus much from you,
I pray desire her call her wisdom to her:
So, fare you well.
If you do chance to hear of that blind traitor,
Preferment falls on him that cuts him off.
Oswald. Would I could meet him, madam: I would show
What party I do follow.
Regan. Fare thee well. [*Exeunt.*

SCENE VI

THE COUNTRY NEAR DOVER

Enter GLOUCESTER, *and* EDGAR *dressed like a peasant.*

Gloucester. When shall I come to the top of that same hill?

ACT IV SCENE VI

    18 charg'd my duty: invoked my sense of duty to her (to deliver the letter at once).

    20 Belike: probably.

    21 love thee much: reward you highly.

    24 at her late being here: when she was here recently.

    25 œilliades: amorous glances. **speaking**: eloquent.

    26 of her bosom: in her confidence.

    28 in understanding: from my own knowledge.

    29 take this note: take note of what I say.

    30 talk'd: come to an understanding.

    31 convenient: fitting. **for my hand**: to be my husband.

    32 gather: infer.

    33 this: a token or letter.

    35 call her ... her: to show some sense (i.e. remember she has a husband).

    38 him that: the man who, whoever.

    39 Would: I wish.

IV. vi

    1 that same hill: see IV. i 73.

Edgar. You do climb up it now; look how we labour.
Gloucester. Methinks the ground is even.
Edgar.   Horrible steep.
   Hark! do you hear the sea?
Gloucester.   No, truly.
5 *Edgar.* Why, then your other senses grow imperfect
   By your eyes' auguish.
Gloucester.   So may it be, indeed.
   Methinks thy voice is alter'd, and thou speak'st
   In better phrase and matter than thou didst.
Edgar. Y'are much deceived; in nothing am I chang'd
10   But in my garments.
Gloucester.   Methinks you're better spoken.
Edgar. Come on, sir; here's the place; stand still.
   How fearful
   And dizzy 'tis to cast one's eyes so low!
   The crows and choughs that wing the midway sir
15 Show scarce so gross as beetles; half way down
   Hangs one that gathers samphire, dreadful trade!
   Methinks he seems no bigger than his head.
   The fishermen that walk upon the beach
   Appear like mice, and yond tall anchoring bark
20 Diminish'd to her cock, her cock a buoy
   Almost too small for sight. The murmuring surge,
   That on the unnumber'd idle pebble chafes,
   Cannot be heard so high. I'll look no more,
   Lest my brain turn, and the deficient sight
25 Topple down headlong.
Gloucester.   Set me where you stand.
Edgar. Give me your hand; you are now within a foot
   Of the extreme verge: for all beneath the moon
   Would I not leap upright.
Gloucester.   Let go my hand.
   Here, friend, 's another purse; in it a jewel

ACT IV SCENE VI

3 Horrible: horribly.

10 better spoken: better in speech (accent, propriety and grace). 注意,Edgar 自本场起用无韵诗讲话。　**spoken** (p.p.): of speech, speaking; e.g. fair-spoken, plain-spoken, well-spoken.

14 choughs: jackdaws, 红嘴山鸦。　**wing**(v.t.): traverse by flying.

15 scarce: hardly.　**gross**: large.

16 one: a man.　**samphire**: 海蓬子(一种生长于欧洲海岩峭壁岸缝间的伞形多肉植物,腌渍后可供食用)。

19 yond: yonder.

20 cock: cock-boat, ship's boat, 舢板。　**buoy**: 浮标。

22 unnumber'd: innumerable.　**pebble**: 在当时的英语中可用作复数。　**chafes**: frets, wears by rubbing.

24 the deficient sight: I, through failing sight.

27—28 for…upright: I would not jump straight up in the air for anything in the world.

29 another purse: see IV. i 64.

Well worth a poor man's taking; fairies and gods
Prosper it with thee! Go thou further off;
Bid me farewell, and let me hear thee going.
Edgar. Now fare you well, good sir.
Gloucester.   With all my heart.
Edgar. Why I do trifle thus with his despair
Is done to cure it.
Gloucester.   O you mighty gods!
This world I do renounce, and, in your sights,
Shake patiently my great affliction off;
If I could bear it longer, and not fall
To quarrel with your great opposeless wills,
My snuff and loathed part of nature should
Burn itself out. If Edgar live, O, bless him!
Now, fellow, fare thee well.

Edgar.   Gone, sir: farewell.
                [GLOUCESTER *falls forward*.
[*Aside*. And yet I know not how conceit may rob
The treasury of life when life itself
Yields to the theft; had he been where he thought
By this had thought been past. Alive or dead?
[*To* GLOUCESTER.] Ho, you sir! friend! Hear you, sir? speak!
Thus might he pass indeed; yet he revives.
What are you, sir?
Gloucester.   Away and let me die.
Edgar. Hadst thou been aught but gossamer, feathers, air,
So many fathom down precipitating,
Thou'dst shiver'd like an egg; but thou dost breathe,
Hast heavy substance, bleed'st not, speak'st, art sound.
Ten masts at each make not the altitude
Which thou hast perpendicularly fell:

ACT IV SCENE VI

31 Prosper it with thee: Make the purse lucky for you (perhaps a reference to a belief that fairies multiplied treasure trove).

34—35 i.e. The purpose of my trifling … is to cure it (his despair).

36 sights: sight, 当时抽象名词可用复数。

38 fall: begin.

39 quarrel with: rebel against. **opposeless**: irresistible.

40—41 i.e. I would let the miserable remnant of my life expire naturally (instead of seeking my own death). **snuff**: half-burnt wick of a candle, 烛花。

43 I know not how: I don't know how it is that. **conceit**: imagination.

44—45 when life … theft: when there is no longer the will to live.

46 By … past: i.e. By this time he would be dead, past thinking about anything.

47 Edgar 现在假装过路人,在悬崖下发现 Gloucester。

48 旁白。 **pass**: die.

49 What: How.

50 aught: anything. **but**: except.

51 fathom: 用作复数。 **precipitating**: falling headlong.

52 Thou'dst shiver'd: You would have smashed to pieces.

54 at each: end to end.

55 fell: fallen.

Thy life's a miracle. Speak yet again.
Gloucester. But have I fallen or no?
Edgar. From the dread summit of this chalky bourn.
Look up a-height; the shrill-gorg'd lark so far
60 Cannot be seen or heard: do but look up.
Gloucester. Alack! I have no eyes.
Is wretchedness depriv'd that benefit
To end itself by death? 'Twas yet some comfort,
When misery could beguile the tyrant's rage,
65 And frustrate his proud will.
Edgar. Give me your arm:
Up: so. How is't? Feel you your legs? You stand.
Gloucester. Too well, too well.
Edgar. This above all strangeness.
Upon the crown o' the cliff, what thing was that
Which parted from you?
Gloucester. A poor unfortunate beggar.
70 *Edgar.* As I stood here below methought his eyes
Were two full moons; he had a thousand noses,
Horns whelk'd and wav'd like the enridged sea:
It was some fiend; therefore, thou happy father,
Think that the clearest gods, who make them honours
75 Of men's impossibilities, have preserv'd thee.
Gloucester. I do remember now; henceforth I'll bear
Affliction till it do cry out itself
'Enough, enough,' and die. That thing you speak of
I took it for a man; often 'twould say
80 'The fiend, the fiend:' he led me to that place.
Edgar. Bear free and patient thoughts. But who comes here?

Enter LEAR, *fantastically dressed with flowers.*

The safer sense will ne'er accommodate
His master thus.

ACT IV SCENE VI

58 dread: dreadful. **chalky**: 白垩岩的; 英格兰多佛海边有高大的白垩岩。 **bourn**: boundary (of the sea) i.e. the cliff.

59 a-height: on high. **shrill-gorg'd**: shrill-throated, high-voiced.

64 beguile: cheat (by death).

72 whelk'd: twisted. **enridged**: ridged, furrowed.

73 happy father: fortunate old man.

74 clearest: purest and most righteous.

74—75 who … impossibilities: who win honour for themselves by doing deeds which are impossible with men.

81 free: free of despair, serene.

82—83 i.e. a man in his right senses would never dress himself up like this. **The safer sense**: a saner mind. **accommodate**: furnish, equip. **His**: Its.

Lear. No, they cannot touch me for coining;
I am the king himself.

Edgar. O thou side-piercing sight!

Lear. Nature's above art in that respect. There's your press-money. That fellow handles his bow like a crow-keeper: draw me a clothier's yard. Look, look! a mouse. Peace, peace! this piece of toasted cheese will do 't. There's my gauntlet; I'll prove it on a giant. Bring up the brown bills. O! well flown, bird; i' the clout, i' the clout: hewgh! Give the word.

Edgar. Sweet marjoram.

Lear. Pass.

Gloucester. I know that voice.

Lear. Ha! Goneril, with a white beard! They flatter'd me like a dog, and told me I had white hairs in my beard ere the black ones were there. To say 'ay' and 'no' to every thing I said! 'Ay' and 'no' too was no good divinity. When the rain came to wet me once and the wind to make me chatter, when the thunder would not peace at my bidding, there I found 'em, there I smelt 'em out. Go to, they are not men o' their words: they told me I was every thing; 'tis a lie, I am not ague-proof.

Gloucester. The trick of that voice I do well remember: Is 't not the king?

Lear.   Ay, every inch a king:
When I do stare, see how the subject quakes.
I pardon that man's life. What was thy cause?
Adultery?
Thou shalt not die: die for adultery! No:
The wren goes to 't, and the small gilded fly
Does lecher in my sight.
Let copulation thrive; for Gloucester's bastard son
Was kinder to his father than my daughters

ACT IV SCENE VI

84 **touch**: punish. **coining**: making of money, minting.

86 **side-piercing**: heart-rending.

87 **Nature's above art**: i.e. A king is above a coiner (issuer of false money).

88 **press-money**: money paid to a man forced into the services (cf. press-gang).

88—89 **crow-keeper**: scarecrow or person hired to drive crows away. **me**: for me to see. 这是 ethical dative 格。 **clothier's yard**: arrow a cloth-yard long.

91 **do 't**: i.e. capture the mouse. **gauntlet**: mailed glove thrown down as a challenge. **prove it on**: support the challenge against.

92 **brown bills**: halberds（钺戟）painted brown or the soldiers carrying them. **bird**: i.e. arrow.

93 **clout**: 靶心。 **hewgh**: 箭在空中飞过时发出的飒飒声。 **word**: password.

94 **marjoram**: 牛至菜,据说是用来治疯狂的一种草药,此处用作口令。

98 **like a dog**: as a dog fawns on people. **white hairs**: i.e. wisdom of age.

99—100 **To say … said**: i.e. To contradict me in nothing.

100—101 **'Ay' … divinity**: It was not good Christian behaviour to say both 'yes' and 'no' (to the same proposition in order to please the speaker). 参看《圣经·新约·雅各书》第 5 章第 12 节:"你们说话,是就说是,不是就说不是,免得你们落在审判之下。"又,《圣经·新约·哥林多后书》第 1 章 19 节:"耶稣基督总没有是而又非的,在他只有一是。"

103 **peace**(v.i.): be still. **found 'em**: found the flatterers out.

104 **Go to**: Come now.

105 **was every thing**: i.e. had every desirable quality.

106 **ague-proof**: proof against fever.

107 **trick**: accent, characteristic quality.

109 **the subject**: my subjects, 集合名词。

110 **cause**: case, accusation.

113 **wren**: 鹪鹩。 **goes to 't**: gives energy and time to doing it (adultery).

114 **lecher**: have sexual intercourse.

Got 'tween the lawful sheets.
To 't luxury, pell-mell! for I lack soldiers.
Behold yond simpering dame.
120 Whose face between her forks presageth snow;
That minces virtue, and does shake the head
To hear of pleasure's name;
The fitchew nor the soiled horse goes to 't
With a more riotous appetite.
125 Down from the waist they are Centaurs,
Though women all above:
But to the girdle do the gods inherit,
Beneath is all the fiends';
There's hell, there's darkness, there is the sulphurous pit,
130 Burning, scalding, stench, consumption; fie, fie, fie! pah, pah! Give me an ounce of civet, good apothecary, to sweeten my imagination: there's money for thee.

Gloucester. O! let me kiss that hand!

Lear. Let me wipe it first; it smells of mortality.

135 *Gloucester.* O ruin'd piece of nature! This great world
Shall so wear out to nought. Dost thou know me?

Lear. I remember thine eyes well enough. Dost thou squiny at me? No, do thy worst, blind Cupid; I'll not love. Read thou this challenge; mark but the penning of it.

140 *Gloucester.* Were all the letters suns I could not see.

Edgar. [*Aside.*] I would not take this from report; it is,
And my heart breaks at it.

Lear. Read.

Gloucester. What! with the case of eyes?

145 *Lear.* O, ho! are you there with me? No eyes in your head, nor no money in your purse? Your eyes are in a

ACT IV SCENE VI

117 **Got**: begotten.

118 **To 't**: go to it,参见 113 行注。 **luxury**: lust. **pell-mell**: promiscuously.

119 **yond**: yonder. **simpering**: smiling in an affected way.

120 **forks**: ①发钗; ②legs. 如为后义,则 between 短语修饰 snow. **presageth snow**: suggests icy chastity.

121 **minces**: affects in a mincing manner.

122 **pleasure's name**: the very name of sexual pleasure.

123 **fitchew**: polecat,臭猫。 **nor**: 用作 or. **soil'd**: overfed.

125 **Centaurs**: 希腊神话中人头马怪物,性淫荡。

127 **But to**: Only as far as. **inherit**: possess, control.

130 **consumption**: rotting.

131 **civet**: perfume,麝香。

134 **mortality**: death.

135 **piece**: work. **piece of nature**: i.e. man.

136 **so**: in the same way, as you have done.

138 **squiny**: squint. **blind Cupid**: 罗马神话中的小爱神,其形象是一个手持弓箭、蒙上双眼的孩童。

139 **mark…of it**: just notice how it is written.

141 **take**: believe. **it is**: it is true.

144 **case**: sockets.

145 **are you…me?**: Is that what you mean?

146—147 **in a heavy case**: in a bad condition. 这里的 case 和下句的 light 都是双关语。

heavy case, your purse in a light: yet you see how this world goes.

Gloucester. I see it feelingly.

150 *Lear.* What! art mad? A man may see how this world goes with no eyes. Look with thine ears: see how yond justice rails upon you simple thief. Hark, in thine ear: change places; and, handy-dandy, which is the justice, which is the thief? Thou hast seen a
155 farmer's dog bark at a beggar?

Gloucester. Ay, sir.

Lear. And the creature run from the cut? There thou mightst behold the great image of authority; a dog's obey'd in office.

160 Thou rascal beadle, hold thy bloody hand!
Why dost thou lash that whore? Strip thine own back;
Thou hotly lusts to use her in that kind
For which thou whipp'st her. The usurer hangs the cozener.
Through tatter'd clothes small vices do appear.
165 Robes and furr'd growns hide all. Plate sin with gold,
And the strong lance of justice hurtless breaks;
Arm it in rags, a pigmy's straw doth pierce it.
None does offend, none, I say none; I'll able 'em:
Take that of me, my friend, who have the power
170 To seal the accuser's lips. Get thee glass eyes;
And, like a scurvy politician, seem
To see the things thou dost not. Now, now, now, now;
Pull off my boots; harder, harder; so.

Edgar. [*Aside.*] O! matter and impertinency mix'd;
175 Reason in madness!

Lear. If thou wilt weep my fortunes, take my eyes;
I know thee well enough; thy name is Gloucester;

ACT IV SCENE VI

149 **feelingly**: ①by sense of feeling; ②with keen emotion.

152 **yond** 和 **you**: over there.　**justice**: judge.　**simple**: poor, humble.

153 **change places**: i.e. get them to change places.　**handy-dandy**: take your choice. 语出儿童猜豆在哪只手中的游戏,意为"翻手之间"。

157 **creature**: human being, i.e. the beggar.

158 **image**: type, example.　**a dog**: even a dog.

159 **in office**: in a position of authority.

160 **beadle**: parish constable who has power to punish small offences.

161 参看《圣经・新约・约翰福音》第8章第7节,耶稣说,谁自己是没有罪的,才可以用石头打一个被捉拿的淫妇。

162 **in that kind**: in the lustful way.

163 **The usurer…cozener**: the judge guilty of usury sentences the petty cheat to be hanged.

165 **Plate sin with gold**: give the sinner the armour of riches. **plate**(v.t.): clothe in plate-armour.

166 **hurtless**: without doing any harm.

168 **able**: vouch for.

171 **scurvy politician**: vile schemer.　**seem**: pretend.

174 **matter**: good sense.　**impertinency**: irrelevance, nonsense.

176 **weep**(v.t.): lament.

Thou must be patient; we came crying hither:
Thou know'st the first time that we small the air
180 We waul and cry. I will preach to thee; mark.
Gloucester. Alack! alack the day!
Lear. When we are born, we cry that we are come
To this great stage of fools. This' a good block!
It were a delicate stratagem to shoe
185 A troop of horse with felt; I'll put it in proof,
And when I have stol'n upon these sons-in-law,
Then, kill, kill, kill, kill, kill, kill!

Enter Gentleman, *with* Attendants.

Gentleman. O! here he is; lay hand upon him. Sir,
Your most dear daughter —
190 *Lear.* No rescue? What! a prisoner? I am even
The natural fool of fortune. Use me well;
You shall have ransom. Let me have surgeons;
I am cut to the brains.
Gentleman. You shall have any thing.
Lear. No seconds? All myself?
195 Why this would make a man a man of salt,
To use his eyes for garden water-pots,
Ay, and laying autumn's dust.
Gentleman. Good sir, —
Lear. I will die bravely as a bridegroom. What!
I will be jovial: come, come; I am a king,
200 My masters, know you that?
Gentleman. You are a royal one, and we obey you.
Lear. Then there's life in it. Nay, an you get it, you
shall get it by running. Sa, sa, sa, sa.
[*Exit.* Attendants *follow.*
Gentleman. A sight most pitiful in the meanest wretch,
205 Past speaking of in a king! Thou hast one daughter,
Who redeems nature from the general curse

178　hither: i.e. into this world.

 180　waul: wail (cf. caterwaul).　**mark**(v.i.): take particular notice.

 183　This': This is.　**block**: 制毡帽用的模子,可能转义为毡帽。

 184　delicate: ingenious.

 185　horse: horses.　**in proof**: to the test.

 186　stol'n upon: crept silently up to.

 191　natural fool of fortune: born to be the sport of fortune.　**Use**: Treat.

 193　cut to the brains: mentally disturbed (cf. 'cut to the heart').

 194　seconds: supporters.

 195　salt: salt tears.

 198　bravely: ①courageously; ②finely clothed.

 202　there's life in it: there's still hope for me.　**an**: if.

 203　Sa, sa: French ça, ça; a cry inciting to action, as to hunting dogs.

 206　nature: human nature.　**general**: universal.

Which twain have brought her to.

Edgar. Hail, gentle sir!

Gentleman. Sir, speed you: what's your will?

Edgar. Do you hear aught, sir, of a battle toward?

210 *Gentleman.* Most sure and vulgar; every one hears that,

Which can distinguish sound.

Edgar. But, by your favour,

How near's the other army?

Gentleman. Near, and on speedy foot; the main descry

Stands on the hourly thought.

Edgar. I thank you, sir: that's all.

215 *Gentleman.* Though that the queen on special cause is here,

Her army is mov'd on.

Edgar. I thank you, sir.

[*Exit* Gentleman.

Gloucester. You ever-gentle gods, take my breath from me:

Let not my worser spirit tempt me again

To die before you please!

Edgar. Well pray you, father.

220 *Gloucester.* Now, good sir, what are you?

Edgar. A most poor man, made tame to fortune's blows;

Who, by the art of known and feeling sorrows,

Am pregnant to good pity. Give me you-hand,

I'll lead you to some biding.

Gloucester. Hearty thanks:

225 The bounty and the benison of heaven

To boot, and boot!

Enter OSWALD.

Oswald. A proclaim'd prize! Most happy!

207 twain: i.e. Goneril and Regan. **her**: i.e. nature.

208 gentle: noble. **speed you**: May God speed (give success to) you.

209 toward: imminent.

210 vulgar: commonly known.

211 Which: Who.

213—214 the main…thought: the sight of the main body is expected any hour.

215 Though that: Although. **on special cause**: for special reason.

218 worser spirit: evil angel.

219 before you please: before a time that pleases the gods.

222 the art…sorrows: the lessons of heartfelt sorrows I have experienced.

223 pregnant to: disposed to show.

224 biding: lodging place.

225 benison: blessing.

226 To boot, and boot: in addition, and may it help you. 两个 boot 意思不同，前者为名词，后者为动词。 **A proclaim'd prize**: a man with a prize on his head. **happy**: lucky.

That eyeless head of thine was first fram'd flesh
To raise my fortunes. Thou old unhappy traitor,
Briefly thyself remember: the sword is out
That must destroy thee.
Gloucester.   Now let thy friendly hand
Put strength enough to 't.   [EDGAR *interposes*.
Oswald.   Wherefore, bold peasant,
Dar'st thou support a publish'd traitor? Hence;
Lest that infection of his fortune take
Like hold on thee. Let go his arm.
Edgar. Chill not let go, zur, without vurther 'casion.
Oswald. Let go, slave, or thou diest.
Edgar. Good gentleman, go your gait, and let poor volk pass. An chud ha' bin zwaggered out of my life, 'twould not ha' bin zo long as 'tis by a vortnight. Nay, come not near th' old man; keep out, che vor ye, or ise try whether your costard or my ballow be the harder. Chill be plain with you.
Oswald. Out, dunghill!
Edgar. Chill pick your teeth, zur. Come; no matter vor your foins.

         [*They fight, and* EDGAR *knocks him down*.
Oswald. Slave, thou hast slain me. Villain, take my purse.
If ever thou wilt thrive, bury my body;
And give the letters which thou find'st about me
To Edmund Earl of Gloucester; seek him out
Upon the English party: O! untimely death.   [*Dies*.
Edgar. I know thee well: a serviceable villain;
As duteous to the vices of thy mistress
As badness would desire.
Gloucester.   What! is he dead?
Edgar. Sit you down, father; rest you.
Let's see his pockets; these letters that he speaks of

ACT IV SCENE VI

227　fram'd：made.

229　thyself remember：remember your sins, prepare for death. **out**：unsheathed.

232　publish'd：proclaimed.

233—234　i.e. lest the same fate overtake you.　**Like**：Similar.

235　Chill：I will. 此处 Edgar 假装农民,用英格兰西南部农村的方言说话。其主要特点是:清辅音[s]和[f]浊化成[z]和[v];保留了源出中古英语 ich(＝I)的一些形式,如 chill＝I will, chud＝I could.　**zur**：sir.　**vurther**：further.　**'casion**：occasion, reason.

236　or：otherwise.

237　gait：way.

238　An...zwaggered：If I could have been bullied.

240—241　che vor ye：I warrant you.　**ise**：I shall.

241　costard：head.　**ballow**：cudgel.

244　pick：knock out.

245　foins：thrusts.

246　Villain：Serf.

250　Upon：on.　**party**：side.

251　serviceable：diligent in service.　**villain**：rascal.

May be my friends. He's dead; I am only sorry
He had no other deaths-man. Let us see:
Leave, gentle wax; and, manners, blame us not:
To know our enemies' minds, we'd rip their hearts;
Their papers, is more lawful.

  'Let our reciprocal vows be remembered. You have many opportunities to cut him off; if your will want not, time and place will be fruitfully offered. There is nothing done if he return the conqueror; then am I the prisoner, and his bed my gaol; from the loathed warmth whereof deliver me, and supply the place for your labour.

  'Your — wife, so I would say —

     'Affectionate servant,
       'GONERIL.'

O undistinguish'd space of woman's will!
A plot upon her virtuous husband's life,
And the exchange my brother! Here, in the sands,
Thee I'll rake up, the post unsanctified
Of murderous lechers; and in the mature time
With this ungracious paper strike the sight
Of the death-practis'd duke. For him 'tis well
That of thy death and business I can tell.

Gloucester. The king is mad: how stiff is my vile sense,
That I stand up, and have ingenious feeling
Of my huge sorrows! Better I were distract:
So should my thoughts be sever'd from my griefs,
And woes by wrong imaginations lose
The knowledge of themselves.   [*Drums afar off.*
Edgar.   Give me your hand:
Far off, methinks, I hear the beaten drum.
Come, father, I'll bestow you with a friend.

            [*Exeunt.*

ACT IV SCENE VI

256 be my friends: help me.

257 deaths-man: executioner.

258 Leave: By your leave (permission), 对不起, 把你拆开了。 **wax**: 指信封上的封蜡。

259 To: In order to.

260 i.e. It is more lawful to rip open their papers.

262 him: i.e. Albany.

262—263 want not: not be deficient.

263 fruitfully: plentifully.

263—264 There…done: i.e. We shall have achieved nothing.

266 whereof: i.e. of his bed.

266—267 for your labour: ①as a reward for your efforts; ②as a place for your amorous labours.

269 servant: professed lover.

271 undistinguish'd: unbounded. **space**: range. **will**: desire, lust.

274 rake up: cover up, bury (by raking sand over the body). **the post**: messenger, postman, 此处为 thee 的同位语。

275 in the mature time: when the time is ripe.

276 ungracious: wicked. **strike**: blast.

277 death-practis'd: whose death is plotted.

278 thy: 指 Oswald 的。同 274 行的 Thee.

279 stiff: unbending, unfeeling. **sense**: mental powers.

280 ingenious feeling: keen consciousness.

281 distract: distracted, mad.

282 i.e. I should not realize my miseries.

283 wrong imaginations: illusions.

286 bestow: lodge.

SCENE VII

A TENT IN THE FRENCH CAMP

Enter CORDELIA, KENT, Doctor, *and* Gentleman.

Cordelia. O thou good Kent! how shall I live and work
   To match thy goodness? My life will be too short,
   And every measure fail me.
Kent. To be acknowledg'd, madam, is o'erpaid.
5   All my reports go with the modest truth,
   Nor more nor clipp'd, but so.
Cordelia.   Be better suited;
   These weeds are memories of those worser hours;
   I prithee, put them off.
Kent.   Pardon me, dear madam;
   Yet to be known shortens my made intent;
10   My boon I make it that you know me not
   Till time and I think meet.
Cordelia. Then be 't so, my good lord. —

                              [*to the* Doctor.]

   How does the king?
Doctor. Madam, sleeps still
Cordelia. O you kind gods,
15   Cure this great breach in his abused nature!
   The untun'd and jarring senses, O! wind up
   Of this child-changed father!
Doctor.   So please your majesty
   That we may wake the king? he hath slept long.
Cordelia. Be govern'd by your knowledge, and proceed
20   I' the sway of your own will. Is he array'd?

   Enter LEAR *in his chair, carried by* Servants.

Gentleman. Ay, madam; in the heaviness of sleep, We
   put fresh garments on him.
Doctor. Be by, good madam, when we do awake him;

ACT IV SCENE VII

IV. vii

   3 **measure**: degree (of gratitude, compared with Kent's services).

   5 **All…truth**: What I have reported to you is a truthful and moderate account.

   6 **Nor more…so**: Neither exaggerated nor understated but exactly as the truth. **suited**: dressed.

   7 **weeds**: shabby clothes. **memories**: reminders.

   9 **Yet…intent**: To reveal my identity at this point would interfere with my prearranged intention.

   10 **boon**: request. My boon 在此句中作宾语补语。

   11 i.e. Till I think the time is appropriate.

   16 **jarring**: discordant. **wind up**: tune (the strings or mechanism, as of a musical instrument).

   17 **child-changed**: changed into a child (in mind). **please**: may it please.

   20 **I' the sway…will**: As you think best. **array'd**: dressed.

I doubt not of his temperance.
Cordelia.   Very well.   [*Music.*
25 *Doctor.* Plesse you, draw near. Louder the music there.
Cordelia. O my dear father! Restoration, hang
Thy medicine on my lips, and let this kiss
Repair those violent harms that my two sisters
Have in thy reverence made!
Kent.   Kind and dear princess!
30 *Cordelia.* Had you not been their father, these white flakes
Had challeng'd pity of them. Was this a face
To be expos'd against the warring winds?
To stand against the deep dread-bolted thunder?
In the most terrible and nimble stroke
35 Of quick cross lightning? to watch — poor perdu! —
With this thin helm? Mine enemy's dog,
Though he had bit me, should have stood that night
Against my fire. And wast thou fain, poor father,
To hovel thee with swine and rogues forlorn,
40 In short and musty straw? Alack, alack!
'Tis wonder that thy life and wits at once
Had not concluded all. He wakes; speak to him.
Doctor. Madam, do you; 'tis fittest.
Cordelia. How does my royal lord? How fares your majesty?
45 *Lear.* You do me wrong to take me out o' the grave;
Thou art a soul in bliss; but I am bound
Upon a wheel of fire, that mine own tears
Do scald like molten lead.
Cordelia.   Sir, do you know me?
Lear. You are a spirit, I know; when did you die?
50 *Cordelia.* Still, still, far wide.
Doctor. He's scarce awake; let him alone awhile.

24 temperance: sanity.

26 Restoration: The power of restoring the senses.

29 reverence: aged and revered person.

30 Had you: Even if you had.   **flakes**: locks of hair.

31 Had challeng'd: Would have claimed.   **of**: from.

33 deep: deep-voiced.   **dread-bolted**: bringing dreaded thunderbolts.

34 nimble: swift.

35 cross: zigzag.   **watch**: stay awake on duty.   **perdu**: sentinel at a dangerous post (French, sentinelle perdue).

36 thin helm: light helmet, i.e. his hair.

37 he: it.   **bit**: bitten.

38 Against: In front of.   **fain**: obliged.

39 To hovel thee: to take shelter in a hovel.   **rogues**: vagabonds.

40 short: scanty and broken up.

42 concluded all: ended altogether.

47 wheel of fire: 传说中地狱里的刑具之一。   **that**: so that.

48 scald: scald me.

50 wide: wide of the mark, astray (in mind).

51 scarce: scarcely.

Lear. Where have I been? Where am I? Fair daylight?
I am mightily abus'd. I should even die with pity
To see another thus. I know not what to say.
55 I will not swear these are my hands: let's see;
I feel this pin prick. Would I were assur'd
Of my condition!
Cordelia. O! look upon me, sir,
And hold your hands in benediction o'er me,
No, sir, you must not kneel.
Lear. Pray, do not mock me:
60 I am a very foolish fond old man,
Fourscore and upward, not an hour more or less;
And, to deal plainly,
I fear I am not in my perfect mind.
Methinks I should know you and know this man;
65 Yet I am doubtful: for I am mainly ignorant
What place this is, and all the skill I have
Remembers not these garments; nor I know not
Where I did lodge last night. Do not laugh at me;
For, as I am a man, I think this lady
70 To be my child Cordelia.
Cordelia. And so I am, I am.
Lear. Be your tears wet? Yes, faith. I pray, weep not:
If you have poison for me, I will drink it.
I know you do not love me; for your sisters
Have, as I do remember, done me wrong:
75 You have some cause, they have not.
Cordelia. No cause, no cause.
Lear. Am I in France?
Kent. In your own kingdom, sir.
Lear. Do not abuse me.
Doctor. Be comforted, good madam; the great rage,

ACT IV SCENE VII

53 abus'd: deceived, deluded.
54 another thus: someone else in this condition.
56 Would: I wish.
60 fond: foolishly loving, credulous.
62 deal plainly: speak frankly.
65 mainly: completely.
66 skill: mental power.
71 faith: by my faith.
75 cause: i.e. cause or reason to do me wrong.
77 abuse: deceive.
78 rage: frenzy, madness.

You see, is kill'd in him; and yet it is danger
80 To make him even o'er the time he has lost.
Desire him to go in; trouble him no more
Till further settling.

Cordelia. Will't please your highness walk?

Lear. You must bear with me.
Pray you now, forget and forgive: I am old and foolish.

[*Exeunt* LEAR, CORDELIA, Doctor, *and* Attendants.

85 *Gentleman.* Holds it true, sir, that the Duke of Cornwall was so slain?

Kent. Most certain, sir.

Gentleman. Who is conductor of his people?

Kent. As 'tis said, the bastard son of Gloucester.

90 *Gentleman.* They say Edgar, his banished son, is with the Earl of Kent in Germany.

Kent. Report is changeable. 'Tis time to look about; the powers of the kingdom approach apace.

Gentleman. The arbitrement is like to be bloody. Fare
95 you well, sir.

Kent. My point and period will be thoroughly wrought,
Or well or ill, as this day's battle's fought. [*Exit.*

79　kill'd: destroyed.

80　even(v.i.): fill up the gap.

82　Till…settling: Till his mind further settles down.

83　walk: withdraw.

84　本场以下各行对折本全删。

85　Holds it true: Is it still held (accepted) to be true.

88　conductor: leader.

92　look about: be wary.

93　powers of the kingdom: British armies.

94　arbitrement: decision (of the war).　**like**: likely.

96　My point…wrought: The conclusion and full stop of my life will be thoroughly brought about.

97　Or: either, whether.　**as**: according as.

ACT V

SCENE I

THE BRITISH CAMP NEAR DOVER

Enter, with drum and colours, EDMUND, REGAN, Officers, Soldiers, *and others.*

Edmund. Know of the duke if his last purpose hold,
Or whether since he is advis'd by aught
To change the course; he's full of alteration
And self-reproving; bring his constant pleasure.
[*To an* Officer, *who goes out.*
5 *Regan.* Our sister's man is certainly miscarried.
Edmund. 'Tis to be doubted, madam.
Regan.   Now, sweet lord,
You know the goodness I intend upon you:
Tell me, but truly, but then speak the truth,
Do you not love my sister
Edmund.   In honour'd love.
10 *Regan.* But have you never found my brother's way
To the forefended place?
Edmund.   That thought abuses you.
Regan. I am doubtful that you have been conjunct
And bosom'd with her, as far as we call hers.
Edmund. No, by mine honour, madam.
15 *Regan.* I never shall endure her: dear my lord,
Be not familiar with her.
Edmund.   Fear me not.
She and the duke her husband!

Enter with drums and colours, ALBANY,
GONERIL, *and* Soldiers.

Goneril. [*Aside.*] I had rather lose the battle than that

V. i

 1 **Know of**: Find out from. **last purpose**: most recent decision. **hold**: still holds good.

 2 **since**: since then. **advis'd by aught**: persuaded by any consideration.

 3 **alteration**: changes.

 4 **constant pleasure**: firm decision.

 5 **Our sister's man**: Oswald. **is … miscarried**: has met with some accident.

 6 **doubted**: feared.

 7 **goodness … you**: good thing I intend to confer upon you.

 8 **then**: even if it is what I fear.

 9 **honour'd**: honourable.

 10 **brother**: i.e. brother-in-law, Albany, Goneril 的丈夫。

 11 **forefended place**: forbidden bed. **abuses**: deceives.

 12 **doubtful**: afraid, suspicious. **conjunct**: conjoined, closely united.

 13 **bosom'd**: taken to the bosom, embraced. **as far … hers**: so that we must needs call you her.

 15 **endure her**: i.e. bear to see her separate us.

 16 **Fear**: distrust.

            sister
            Should loosen him and me.
20   *Albany.* Our very loving sister, well be-met.
            Sir, this I heard, the king is come to his daughter,
            With others, whom the rigour of our state
            Forc'd to cry out. Where I could not be honest
            I never yet was valiant; for this business,
25   It toucheth us, as France invades our land,
            Not bolds the king, with others, whom, I fear,
            Most just and heavy causes make oppose.
        Edmund. Sir, you speak nobly.
        Regan.   Why is this reason'd?
        Goneril. Combine together 'gainst the enemy
30   For these domestic and particular broils
            Are not the question here.
        Albany.   Let's then determine
            With the ancient of war on our proceeding.
        Edmund. I shall attend you presently at your tent.
        Regan. Sister, you'll go with us?
35   *Goneril.* No.
        Regan. 'Tis most convenient; pray you, go with us.
        Goneril. [*Aside.*] O, ho! I know the riddle.
            [*Aloud.*] I will go.

                    Enter EDGAR, *disguised.*

        Edgar. If e'er your Grace had speech with man so poor,
            Hear me one word.
        Albany.   I'll overtake you. Speak.
                    [*Exeunt* EDMUND, REGAN, GONERIL, Officers,
                                            Soldiers, *and* Attendants.
40   *Edgar.* Before you fight the battle, ope this letter
            If you have victory, let the trumpet sound
            For him that brought it: wretched though I seem,
            I can produce a champion that will prove

ACT V SCENE I

19 **loosen**: separate. **him**: i.e. Edmund.
20 **be-met**: met.
22 **rigour**: harshness. **our state**: our rule.
23 **cry out**: protest, complain loudly.
24 **for**: as for.
25 **toucheth us, as**: concerns me in so far as.
26 **Not bolds**: not because France emboldens the king (Lear). **with**: and.
26—27 **whom...oppose**: who, I fear, have good and weighty reasons for taking up arms against us.
28 **reason'd**: discussed.
30 **particular broils**: private quarrels.
31 **question**: subject of contention, issue.
32 **the ancient of war**: veteran soldiers.
33 **presently**: at once.
36 **convenient**: proper, befitting.
37 **the riddle**: i.e. what you are after.
38 **had speech**: would deign to speak.
40 **ope**: open.
41 **sound**: i.e. sound a summons.
42 **it**: i.e. the letter.

What is avouched there. If you miscarry,
45 Your business of the world hath so an end,
And machination ceases. Fortune love you!
Albany. Stay till I have read the letter.
Edgar.   I was forbid it.
When time shall serve, let but the herald cry,
And I'll appear again.
50 *Albany.* Why, fare thee well; I will o'erlook thy paper.

Re-enter EDMUND.

Edmund. The enemy's in view; draw up your powers.
Here is the guess of their true strength and froces
By diligent discovery; but your haste
Is now urg'd on you.
Albany.   We will greet the time.   [*Exit.*
55 *Edmund.* To both these sisters have I sworn my love;
Each jealous of the other, as the stung
Are of the adder. Which of them shall I take?
Both? one? or neither? Neither can be enjoy'd
If both remain alive: to take the widow
60 Exasperates, makes mad her sister Goneril;
And hardly shall I carry out my side,
Her husband being alive. Now then, we'll use
His countenance for the battle; which being done,
Let her who would be rid of him devise
65 His speedy taking off. As for the mercy
Which he intends to Lear, and to Cordelia,
The battle done, and they within our power,
Shall never see his pardon; for my state
Stands on me to defend, not to debate.   [*Exit.*

ACT V SCENE I

44 avouched: asserted. **miscarry**: come to grief, fail in battle.

45 Your ... world: your worldly concerns, your life. **so**: in this way.

46 machination: plotting, i.e. Edmund's. **love**: favour. 此句前省略 may.

47 forbid it: forbidden to do so.

50 o'erlook: look at, read through.

51 in view: in sight. **powers**: troops.

52 guess: estimate.

53 discovery: inquiry, reconnoitring.

54 greet the time: go to meet the occasion or emergency.

56 jealous: suspicious. **stung**: p.p. of sting, those who have been bitten.

57 adder: 小毒蛇。

61 hardly: with difficulty. **carry out my side**: win my game（打牌用语）.

63 countenance: authority, prestige.

65 taking off: removal, murder (a euphemism).

66 intends to: intends to show or give to.

68 Shall: They shall. **state**: position.

69 Stands on: Depends on, requires.

SCENE II

A FIELD BETWEEN THE TWO CAMPS

Alarum within. Enter, with drum and colours, LEAR,
CORDELIA, *and their Forces; and exeunt. Enter*
EDGAR *and* GLOUCESTER.

Edgar. Here, father, take the shadow of this tree
For your good host; pray that the right may thrive.
If ever I return to you again,
I'll bring you comfort.
Gloucester. Grace go with you, sir!
[*Exit* EDGAR.

Alarum; afterwards a retreat. Re-enter EDGAR.

5 *Edgar.* Away, old man! give me thy hand; away!
King Lear hath lost, he and his daughter ta'en.
Give me thy hand; come on.
Gloucester. No further, sir; a man may rot even here.
Edgar. What! in ill thoughts again? Men must endure
10 Their going hence, even as their coming hither:
Ripeness is all. Come on.
Gloucester. And that's true too. [*Exeunt.*

SCENE III

THE BRITISH CAMP, NEAR DOVER

Enter, in conquest, with drum and colours,
EDMUND; LEAR *and* CORDELIA,
prisoners; Officers, Soldiers, &c.

Edmund. Some officers take them away: good guard,
Until their greater pleasures first be known
That are to censure them.

ACT V SCENE III

V. ii

    s.d. Alarum: trumpet signal to advance.

    2 host: shelterer.

    4 comfort: consolation. **Grace**: May the grace of God.

    s.d. retreat: trumpet signal to withdraw.

    6 ta'en: taken, captured.

    9 in ill thoughts: despondent. **endure**: wait for, live patiently until.

    11 Ripeness is all: the important thing is to be ready for death when it does come.

V. iii

    1 good guard: keep good guard over them.

    2—3 their greater pleasures ... That: the will of those higher authorities (Albany, &c.) who. **censure**: judge.

Cordelia.   We are not the first
Who, with best meaning, have incurr'd the worst.
5   For thee, oppressed king, am I cast down;
Myself could else out-frown false Fortune's frown.
Shall we not see these daughters and these sisters?
Lear. No, no, no, no! Come, let's away to prison;
We two alone will sing like birds i' the cage:
10 When thou dost ask me blessing, I'll kneel down,
And ask of thee forgiveness: so we'll live,
And pray, and sing, and tell old tales, and laugh
At gilded butterflies, and hear poor rogues
Talk of court news; and we'll talk with them too,
15 Who loses and who wins; who's in, who's out;
And take upon 's the mystery of things,
As if we were God's spies: and we'll wear out,
In a wall'd prison, packs and sects of great ones
That ebb and flow by the moon.
Edmund.   Take them away.
20 *Lear.* Upon such sacrifices, my Cordelia,
The gods themselves throw incense. Have I cautht thee?
He that parts us shall bring a brand from heaven,
And fire us hence like foxes. Wipe thine eyes;
The good years shall devour them, flesh and fell,
25 Ere they shall make us weep: we'll see 'em starve first.
Come.   [*Exeunt* LEAR *and* CORDELIA, *guarded*.
Edmund. Come hither, captain; hark,
Take thou this note; [*Giving a paper.*] go follow them to prison:
One step I have advanc'd thee; if thou dost
30 As this instructs thee, thou dost make thy way
To noble fortunes; know thou this, that men
Are as the time is; to be tender-minded

ACT V SCENE III

4　meaning：intention.

5　cast down：distressed.

6　out-frown … frown：defy misfortune.

8　away：前省略 go.

9　cage：双关语 1. 鸟笼；2. 监狱。

13　gilded butterflies：可能也指 gay courtiers.

16—17　i.e. pretend to know the mystery of Gods' ways as if we were their agents.

17　wear out：outlast, survive.

18—19　packs … moon：cliques and factions of powerful people who rise and fall like tides influenced by the moon.

20　such sacrifices：i.e. as our misfortunes.

21　i.e. gods throw incense upon sacrifices. 表示悦纳祭品。
Have I caught thee：my heavenly jewel? 是 Philip Sideny：Astrophel and Stella (1591) 诗中的一行。Shakespeare 将其作为歌词引用，除这里外，在《温莎的风流娘儿们》III. iii 45 处也曾引用。李尔仍有些语无伦次。

22—23　i.e. it would take a torch from heaven to smoke us out of our prison refuge as foxes are smoked out of their caves.　**shall**：must, have to.

24　The good years：the plague, the devil.　**flesh and fell**：flesh and skin, altogether.

29　advanc'd：promoted.

32　the time：the times, 时务。

Does not become a sword; thy great employment
Will not bear question; either say thou'lt do 't,
35 Or thrive by other means.
Officer. I'll do 't, my lord.
Edmund. About it; and write happy when thou hast done.
Mark, — I say, instantly, and carry it so
As I have set it down.
Officer. I cannot draw a cart nor eat dried oats;
40 If it be man's work I will do it. [*Exit.*

Flourish. Enter ALBANY, GONERIL, REGAN,
Officers, *and* Attendants.

Albany. Sir, you have show'd to-day your valiant strain,
And fortune led you well; you have the captives
Who were the opposites of this day's strife;
I do require them of you, so to use them
45 As we shall find their merits and our safety
May equally determine.
Edmund. Sir, I thought it fit
To send the old and miserable king
To some retention, and appointed guard;
Whose age has charms in it, whose title more,
50 To pluck the common bosom on his side,
And turn our impress'd lances in our eyes
Which do command them. With him I sent the queen;
My reason all the same; and they are ready
To-morrow, or at further space, to appear
55 Where you shall hold your session. At this time
We sweat and bleed; the friend hath lost his friend,
And the best quarrels, in the heat, are curs'd
By those that feel their sharpness;

ACT V SCENE III

33 a sword: i.e. a soldier (who wields a sword).

34 question: argument, discussion. **thou'lt**: thou wilt, you will.

36 About it: Go about it; Get to work on it. **write happy**: call yourself lucky.

37 carry: manage.

39 I...oats: i.e. I am not a horse.

41 strain: disposition.

43 the opposites of: our opponents in.

44 require...you: want them from you. **so to use them**: in order to deal with them in such a way.

45 we: royal we. **merits**: deserts.

48 retention: detention, confinement.

49 Whose: The old king's.

50 pluck...side: win the hearts of the common people over to his side.

51 our impress'd lances: the soldiers (bearers of lances) we had conscripted, or the weapons of our conscripts.

51—52 in our eyes/Which: against ourselves who.

52 the queen: i.e. of France, Cordelia.

54 at further space: later. **space**: time.

57 the best quarrels: quarrels for the best reason. **in the heat** (of the moment): before passions have cooled.

58 their: i.e. of the quarrels.

The question of Cordelia and her father
Requires a fitter place.

Albany.   Sir, by your patience,
I hold you but a subject of this war,
Not as a brother.

Regan.   That's as we list to grace him:
Methinks our pleasure might have been demanded,
Ere you had spoke so far. He led our powers,
Bore the commission of my place and person;
The which immediacy may well stand up,
And call itself your brother.

Goneril.   Not so hot;
In his own grace he doth exalt himself
More than in your addition.

Regan.   In my rights,
By me invested, he compeers the best.

Goneril. That were the most, if he should husband you.

Regan. Jesters do oft prove prophets.

Goneril.   Holla, holla!
That eye that told you so look'd but a-squint.

Regan. Lady, I am not well; else I should answer
From a full-flowing stomach. General,
Take thou my soldiers, prisoners, patrimony;
Dispose of them, of me; the walls are thine;
Witness the world, that I create thee here
My lord and master.

Goneril.   Mean you to enjoy him?

Albany. The let-alone lies not in your good will.

Edmund. Nor in thine, lord.

Albany.   Half-blooded fellow, yes.

Regan. [*To* EDMUND.] Let the drum strike, and prove my title thine.

Albany. Stay yet; hear reason. Edmund, I arrest thee

ACT V SCENE III

60 patience: indulgence, permission.

61 hold: regard as.   **subject of**: subordinate in.

62 brother: colleague.   **we**: royal we.   **list**: are pleased, choose.

63 demanded: asked about.

64 Ere: before.   **spoke**: spoken.   **so far**: so much.

65 commission: mandate.   **place**: position.

66 The which: Which.   **immediacy**: close connection.

67 Not so hot: Don't be in such a hurry.

68 grace: merit.

69 your addition: the title you give him.

70 compeers: equals.

71 That were the most: That investiture would be the most complete.

72 Jesters: people who say things in jest.

73 a-squint: asquint, 斜视。参看英谚 Love being jealous, makes a good eye look asquint.

74 else: otherwise.

75 full-flowing stomach: anger with a full tide of words. 当时人认为胃生怒。

76 patrimony: inheritance from father.

77 the walls are thine: i.e. the fortress (of my body and heart) is yours.

78 Witness the world: Let the world witness.

79 Mean you: Do you intend to.

80 let-alone: refraining from interference, hence permission.

81 Half-blooded fellow: bastard.

82 strike: strike up.   **prove**: demonstrate, establish.

On capital treason; and, in thy attaint,
This gilded serpent. [*Pointing to* GONERIL.] For your claim, fair sister,
I bar it in the interest of my wife;
'Tis she is sub-contracted to this lord,
And I, her husband, contradict your bans.
If you will marry, make your love to me,
My lady is bespoke.
Goneril.   An interlude!
Albany. Thou art arm'd, Gloucester; let the trumpet sound:
If none appear to prove upon thy person
Thy heinous, manifest, and many treasons,
There is my pledge; [*Throws down a glove.*] I'll prove it on thy heart,
Ere I taste bread, thou art in nothing less
Than I have here proclaim'd thee.
Regan.   Sick! O sick!
Goneril. [*Aside.*] If not, I'll ne'er trust medicine.
Edmund. There's my exchange: [*Throws down a glove.*] what in the world he is
That names me traitor, villain-like he lies.
Call by thy trumpet: he that dares approach,
On him, on you, who not? I will maintain
My truth and honour firmly.
Albany. A herald, ho!
Edmund.   A herald, ho! a herald!
Albany. Trust to thy single virtue; for thy soldiers,
All levied in my name, have in my name
Took their discharge.
Regan.   My sickness grows upon me.
Albany. She is not well; convey her to my tent.
                              [*Exit* REGAN, *led.*

84　attaint: impeachment.
85　gilded: gilded-over, fair-seeming.　**For**: As for.
87　is: 前省略 who.　**sub-contracted**: betrothed for the second time.
88　bans: banns, 教堂里的婚事预告, 若有人提出异议可阻其进行。
89　make your love to: court.
90　bespoke: bespoken, engaged, contracted already.　**interlude**: farce, 原义是穿插在长剧幕间的滑稽小品或歌舞表演。
94　pledge: 挑战的信物。
95　Ere … bread: before I have another meal.　**in nothing less**: in no way less guilty.
97　medicine: euphemism for 'poison'.
98　what: whoever.
101　maintain: defend, justify.
104　single virtue: unaided valour.
106　Took: taken.　**Took their discharge**: been discharged or dismissed.

Come hither, herald, —

Enter a Herald.

Let the trumpet sound, —
And read out this.

110 *Officer.* Sound, trumpet! [*A trumpet sounds.*
Herald. 'If any man of quality or degree within the lists
of the army will maintain upon Edmund, supposed
Earl of Gloucester, that he is a manifold traitor, let
him appear at the third sound of the trumpet. He is
bold in his defence.'

115 *Edmund.* Sound! [*First Trumpet.*
Herald. Again! [*Second Trumpet.*
Herald. Again! [*Third Trumpet.*
[*Trumpet answers within.*

Enter EDGAR, *armed, with a Trumpet before him.*

Albany. Ask him his purposes, why he appears
Upon this call o' the trumpet.
Herald. What are you?
120 Your name? your quality? and why you answer
This present summons?
Edgar. Know, my name is lost;
By treason's tooth bare-gnawn and canker-bit;
Yet am I noble as the adversary
I come to cope.
Albany. Which is that adversary?
125 *Edgar.* What 's he that speaks for Edmund Earl of
Gloucester?
Edmund. Himself: what sayst thou to him?
Edgar. Draw thy sword,
That, if my speech offend a noble heart,
Thy arm may do thee justice; here is mine:
Behold, it is the privilege of mine honours,

ACT V SCENE III

111 **quality or degree:** noble birth or rank. **lists:** role, muster.
112 **maintain upon:** assert against. **supposed:** pretended.
113 **manifold traitor:** traitor in many respects.
117 **s.d. with … him:** preceded by a trumpeter.
120 **quality:** rank.
122 **bare-gnawn:** gnawed bare. **canker-bit:** worm-eaten.
124 **cope:** meet in combat. **which:** who.
127 **That:** So that.
129 **it:** to fight, to maintain the truth of my assertion. **mine honours:** my rank.

130 My oath, and my profession: I protest,
Maugre thy strength, youth, place, and eminence,
Despite thy victor sword and fire-new fortune,
Thy valour and thy heart, thou art a traitor,
False to thy gods, thy brother, and thy father,
135 Conspirant 'gainst this high illustrious prince,
And, from the extremest upward of thy head
To the descent and dust below thy foot,
A most toad-spotted traitor. Say thou 'No'.
This sword, this arm, and my best spirits are bent
140 To prove upon thy heart, whereto I speak,
Thou liest.
Edmund. In wisdom I should ask thy name;
But since thy outside looks so fair and warlike,
And that thy tongue some say of breeding breathes,
What safe and nicely I might well delay.
145 By rule of knighthood, I disdain and spurn;
Back do I toss these treasons to thy head,
With the hell-hated lie o'erwhelm thy heart,
Which, for they yet glance by and scarcely bruise,
This sword of mine shall give them instant way,
150 Where they shall rest for ever. Trumpets, speak!
[*Alarums. They fight.* EDMUND *falls.*
Albany. Save him, save him!
Goneril.   This is practice, Gloucester:
By the law of arms thou wast not bound to answer
An unknown opposite; thou art not vanquish'd.
But cozen'd and beguil'd.
Albany.   Shut your mouth, dame,
155 Or with this paper shall I stop it. Hold, sir;
Thou worse than any name, read thine own evil:
No tearing, lady; I perceive you know it.
Goneril. Say, if I do, the laws are mine, not thine:
Who can arraign me for 't?

ACT V SCENE III

130 my profession: i.e. knighthood. **protest**: proclaim that.

131 Maugre: In spite of, French malgré.

132 victor: victorious. **fire-new**: brand-new.

133 heart: courage.

135 Conspirant: Conspiring.

136 upward: top.

137 descent: lowest part.

138 toad-spotted: covered with shame as a toad with spots. **Say thou**: if you say.

139 bent: prepared, ready for action.

140 whereto: to which (your heart).

141 In wisdom: If I were wise.

142 outside: outward appearance.

143 that: since. **say**: assay 的变体, proof, trace.

144 What: i.e. The combat. **safe**(adv.): safely, prudently. **nicely**: with technical correctness. **delay**: put off.

145 I disdain and spurn: I scorn (to delay).

146 treasons: accusations of treason. **to thy head**: in your teeth.

147 hell-hated: hated like hell.

148 Which: 指 treasons. **for**: because. **yet**: only. **glance by**: fly off.

149 give them ... way: open a direct passage into your heart for them.

150 speak(v.i.): sound.

151 Save: Spare. **practice**: trickery.

153 opposite: opponent.

154 cozen'd: tricked. **beguil'd**: cheated.

155 this paper: the letter from Goneril to Edmund. **stop**: stopper, gag. **Hold**: Wait a moment.

156 Thou: 指 Goneril.

158 Say, if: Suppose.

Albany.   Most monstrous!

160   Know'st thou this paper?

Goneril.   Ask me not what I know.
                                                        [*Exit.*

Albany. Go after her; she's desperate; govern her.
                                                  [*Exit an* Officer.

Edmund. What you have charg'd me with, that have I done,

And more, much more; the time will bring it out:

'Tis past, and so am I. But what art thou

165   That hast this fortune on me? If thou'rt noble,

I do forgive thee.

Edgar.   Let's exchange charity.

I am no less in blood than thou art, Edmund;

If more, the more thou hast wrong'd me.

My name is Edgar, and thy father's son.

170   The gods are just, and of our pleasant vices

Make instruments to plague us:

The dark and vicious place where thee he got

Cost him his eyes.

Edmund.   Thou hast spoken right, 'tis true;

The wheel is come full circle; I am here.

175 *Albany.* Methought thy very gait did prophesy

A royal nobleness: I must embrace thee:

Let sorrow split my heart, if ever I

Did hate thee or thy father.

Edgar.   Worthy prince, I know 't.

Albany. Where have you hid yourself?

180   How have you known the miseries of your father?

Edgar. By nursing them, my lord. List a brief tale;

And, when 'tis told, O that my heart would burst!

The bloody proclamation to escape

That follow'd me so near, — O! our lives' sweetness,

185   That we the pain of death would hourly die

ACT V SCENE III

161　govern: control, restrain.

165　fortune on me: lucky victory over me.

166　charity: forgiveness.

167　less in blood: lower in birth.

168　more: higher.

170　pleasant: pleasurable.

171　plague: punish.

172　place: i.e. bed of adultery.　**thee he got**: he (Gloucester) begot you.

174　wheel: wheel of fortune. 中世纪以轮喻命运，人在轮上，或升或降，转了一圈，复归原地。　**here**: ①on the ground, mortally wounded; ②at the lowest point on the wheel.

175　prophesy: indicate.

179　hid: hidden.

181　List: Listen to.

183　to escape: 不定式短语作句子的主语，其宾语是 the bloody proclamation，其谓语是 186 行的 taught.

184—186　our lives'…at once: i.e. life is so sweet that we prefer to suffer the fear of death hourly rather than die at once.

Rather than die at once! — taught me to shift
Into a madamn's rags, to assume a semblance
That very dogs disdain'd: and in this habit
Me I my father with his bleeding rings,
190 Their precious stones new lost; became his guide,
Led him, begg'd for him, sav'd him from despair;
Never, — O fault! — reveal'd myself unto him,
Until some half hour past, when I was arm'd;
Not sure, though hoping, of this good success,
195 I ask'd his blessing, and from fisrt to last
Told him my pilgrimage: but his flaw'd heart, —
Alack! too weak the conflict to support;
'Twixt two extremes of passion, joy and grief,
Burst smilingly.
Edmund.   This speech of yours hath mov'd me,
200 And shall perchance do good; but speak you on;
You look as you had something more to say.
Albany. If there be more, more woeful, hold it in;
For I am almost ready to dissolve,
Hearing of this.
Edgar.   This would have seem'd a period
205 To such as love not sorrow; but another,
To amplify too much, would make much more,
And top extremity.
Whilst I was big in clamour came there a man,
Who, having seen me in my worst estate,
210 Shunn'd my abhorr'd society; but then, finding
Who 'twas that so endur'd, with his strong arms
He fasten'd on my neck, and bellow'd out
As he'd burst heaven; threw him on my father;
Told the most piteous tale of Lear and him
215 That ever ear receiv'd; which in recounting
His grief grew puissant, and the strings of life
Began to crack: twice then the trumpet sounded,

ACT V SCENE III

186 **shift**: change.
188 **very**: even. **habit**: clothing.
189 **rings**: eye-sockets.
190 **stones**: eye-balls. **new**: newly.
192 **fault**: mistake.
194 **success**: outcome.
196 **flaw'd**: cracked.
201 **as**: as if.
202 **hold it in**: keep it back.
203 **dissolve**: i.e. into tears.
204 **period**: limit, ending.

205—207 **but … extremity**: i.e. yet another sorrow, described in full, would exceed the limit.

208 **big in clamour**: loud in lamentation.
209 **estate**: state.
212 **fasten'd … neck**: i.e. embraced me.
213 **As**: As if. **him**: himself.
215 **which**: 指 tale.
216 **puissant**: (too) powerful. **strings of life**: heartstrings.

And there I left him tranc'd.

Albany.   But who was this?

Edgar. Kent, sir, the banish'd Kent; who in disguise
Follow'd his enemy king, and did him service
Improper for a slave.

    Enter a Gentleman, *with a bloody knife.*

Gentleman. Help, help! O help!

Edgar.   What kind of help?

Albany.   Speak, man.

Edgar. What means that bloody knife?

Gentleman.   'Tis hot, it smokes;
It came even from the heart of — O! she's dead.

Albany. Who dead? speak, man.

Gentleman. Your lady, sir, your lady: and her sister
By her is poison'd; she confesses it.

Edmund. I was contracted to them both: all three
Now marry in an instant.

Edgar.   Here comes Kent.

Albany. Produce the bodies, be they alive or dead:
This judgment of the heavens, that makes us tremble,
Touches us not with pity.   [*Exit* Gentleman

    Enter KENT.

                O! is this he?
The time will not allow the compliment
Which very manners urges.

Kent.   I am come
To bid my king and master aye good-night;
Is he not here?

Albany.   Great thing of us forgot!
Speak, Edmund, where's the king? and where's Cordelia?

- 218 **tranc'd**: in a trance, unconscious.
- 220 **enemy**: hostile.
- 221 **Improper for**: Too humble even for.
- 223 **smokes**: steams.
- 228 **contracted**: engaged.
- 230 **Produce**: Bring in.
- 233 **compliment**: formal courtesy, ceremony.
- 234 **very**: mere. **manners**: 用作单数,所以动词用 urges.
- 235 **aye**: for ever.
- 236 **Great…forgot!**: (That is an) important matter forgotten by us.

KING LEAR

Seest thou this object, Kent.

[*The bodies of* GONERIL *and* REGAN *are brought in.*

Kent. Alack! why thus?

Edmund.   Yet Edmund was belov'd:
240 The one the other poison'd for my sake,
And after slew herself.

Albany. Even so. Cover their faces.

Edmund. I pant for life: some good I mean to do
Despite of mine own nature. Quickly send,
245 Be brief in it, to the castle; for my writ
Is on the life of Lear and on Cordelia.
Nay, send in time.

Albany.   Run, run! O run!

Edgar. To whom, my lord? Who has the office? send
Thy token of reprieve.

250 *Edmund.* Well thought on: take my sword,
Give it the captain.

Albany.   Haste thee, for thy life. [*Exit* EDGAR.

Edmund. He hath commission from thy wife and me
To hang Cordelia in the prison, and
To lay the blame upon her own despair,
255 That she fordid herself.

Albany. The gods defend her! Bear him hence awhile.

[EDMUND *is borne off.*

Enter LEAR, *with* CORDELIA *dead in his arms*;
EDGAR, Officer, *and others.*

Lear. Howl, howl, howl, howl! — O, you are men of stones:
Had I your tongues and eyes, I'd use them so
That heaven's vaults should crack. She's gone for ever.
260 I know when one is dead, and when one lives;
She's dead as earth. Lend me a looking-glass;

ACT V SCENE III

238 **object**: sight.
241 **after**: afterwards.
243 **pant for life**: struggle to live a little longer.
245 **writ**: written order.
247 **Nay**: for emphasis, not negation.
248 **office**: commission to carry out the orders.
255 **That**: i.e. So that it might appear that. **fordid**: destroyed.
258 **so**: in such a way.

If that her breath will mist or stain the stone,
Why, then she lives.

Kent.   Is this the promis'd end?

Edgar. Or image of that horror?

Albany.   Fall and cease!

265 *Lear*. This feather stirs; she lives! if it be so,
It is a chance which does redeem all sorrows
That ever I have felt.

Kent. [*Kneeling*.] O, my good master!

Lear. Prithee, away.

Edgar.   'Tis noble Kent, your friend.

Lear. A plague upon you, murderers, traitors all!
270 I might have sav'd her; now, she's gone for ever!
Coredlia, Cordelia! stay a little. Ha!
What is't thou sayst? Her voice was ever soft,
Gentle and low, an excellent thing in woman.
I kill'd the slave that was a-hanging thee.

275 *Officer*. 'Tis true, my lord, he did.

Lear.   Did I not, fellow?
I have seen the day, with my good biting falchion
I would have made them skip: I am old now,
And these same crosses spoil me. Who are you?
Mine eyes are not o' the best: I'll tell you straight.

280 *Kent*. If fortune brag of two she lov'd and hated,
One of them we behold.

Lear. This is a dull sight. Are you not Kent?

Kent.   The same,
Your servant Kent. Where is your servant Caius?

Lear. He's a good fellow, I can tell you that;
285 He'll strike, and quickly too. He's dead and rotten.

Kent. No, my good lord; I am the very man —

Lear. I'll see that straight.

Kent. That, from your first of differnece and decay,
Have follow'd your sad steps.

ACT V SCENE III 239

262 stone：crystal surface of a mirror, 水晶石磨成的镜子。

263 the promis'd end：指《圣经》中预言的世界末日。

264 image：copy, reproduction.　**Fall and cease!**：Let the heavens fall and all things come to an end!

274 a-hanging：a- 系从 on 变来,早期英语中意为 in the act of.

276 falchion：curved light sword.

277 skip：jump, run away.

278 crosses：sufferings.　**spoil me**：wear me down.

279 straight：straightway, in a moment.

280—281 If … behold：Kent 的意思是,你我都是受命运捉弄的人。

282 dull：①dismal, gloomy；②dim, cloudy.

283 Caius：Kent 乔装为奴时用的名字。

287 see that straight：attend to that in a moment.

288 your first of difference and decay：the beginning of your change and decline of fortunes.

Lear. You are welcome hither.
Kent. Nor no man else; all 's cheerless, dark, and deadly
Your eldest daughters have fordone themselves,
And desperately are dead.
Lear. Ay, so I think.
Albany. He knows not what he says, and vain it is
That we present us to him.
Edgar. Very bootless.

Enter an Officer.

Officer. Edmund is dead, my lord.
Albany. That's but a trifle here.
You lords and noble friends, know our intent;
What comfort to this great decay may come
Shall be applied: for us, we will resign,
During the life of this old majesty,
To him our absolute power: — [*To* EDGAR *and* KENT.] You, to your rights;
With boot and such addition as your honours
Have more than merited. All friends shall taste
The wages of their virtue, and all foes
The cup of their deservings. O! see, see!
Lear. And my poor fool is hang'd! No, no, no life!
Why should a dog, a horse, a rat, have life,
And thou no breath at all? Thou'lt come no more,
Never, never, never, never, never!
Pray you, undo this button: thank you, sir.
Do you see this? Look on her, look, her lips,
Look there, look there! [*Dies.*
Edgar. He faints! — my lord, my lord!
Kent. Break, heart; I prithee, break.
Edgar. Look up, my lord.
Kent. Vex not his ghost: O! let him pass; he hates

ACT V SCENE III

290　Nor … else: ①No other man followed you; ② I am the very man.

291　fordone: destroyed.

292　desperately: in despair.

294　present us: present ourselves, i.e. draw his attention to us. **bootless**: useless.

297　What: Whatever.　**this great decay**: this ruin of greatness, i.e. Lear.

298　for: as for.　**resign**: yield, make over.

300　You … rights: You are restored to the positions which are yours by right.

301　boot: profit, advantage.　**addition**: additional marks of distinction.　**honours**: honourable deeds.

302　taste: enjoy, experience.

303　wages: rewards.

304　cup: 苦酒,这个意象的来源是耶稣所受的苦难,叫做杯,见《圣经·新约·马太福音》第26章第39—42节。

305　poor fool: (term of endearment) Cordelia.

313　ghost: departing spirit.　**him**: anyone.

    him
    That would upon the rack of this tough world
315 Stretch him out longer.
  Edgar.   He is gone, indeed.
  Kent. The wonder is he hath endur'd so long:
    He but usurp'd his life.
  Albany. Bear them from hence. Our present business
    Is general woe. [*To* KENT *and* EDGAR.] Friends of
      my soul, you twain
320 Rule in this realm, and the gor'd state sustain.
  Kent. I have a journey, sir, shortly to go;
    My master calls me, I must not say no.
  Edgar. The weight of this sad time we must obey;
    Speak what we feel, not what we ought to say.
325 The oldest hath borne most: we that are young
    Shall never see so much, nor live so long.

          [*Exeunt, with a dead march.*

314　rack：拉肢刑架，中世纪的一种刑具。谓人生痛苦，有如上刑。

317　usurp'd his life：barely or unnaturally maintained his life.

320　gor'd：wounded.

323　obey：accept.

图书在版编目(CIP)数据

李尔王 / (英)莎士比亚(Shakespeare, W.)著；张信威注释. —北京：商务印书馆，2014(2016.3 重印)
(莎翁戏剧经典)
ISBN 978-7-100-09957-8

Ⅰ. ①李… Ⅱ. ①莎… ②张… Ⅲ. ①英语—语言读物 ②剧本—英国—中世纪 Ⅳ. ①H319.4：I

中国版本图书馆 CIP 数据核字(2013)第 095851 号

所有权利保留。
未经许可，不得以任何方式使用。

莎翁戏剧经典
LǏ ĚR WÁNG
李 尔 王
〔英〕威廉·莎士比亚 著

张信威 注释

商 务 印 书 馆 出 版
(北京王府井大街36号 邮政编码 100710)
商 务 印 书 馆 发 行
北 京 冠 中 印 刷 厂 印 刷
ISBN 978-7-100-09957-8

2014 年 8 月第 1 版	开本 787×1092 1/32
2016 年 3 月北京第 2 次印刷	印张 9⅓ 插页 1

定价：28.00 元